HARVARD DISSERTATIONS IN AMERICAN AND ENGLISH LITERATURE

Edited by
STEPHEN ORGEL
Stanford University

A Garland Series

THE EARLY PROSE
OF
WILLIAM CARLOS WILLIAMS
1917-1925

GEOFFREY H. MOVIUS

Garland Publishing, Inc.
New York & London
1987

Library of Congress Cataloging-in-Publication Data

Movius, Geoffrey H. (Geoffrey Hallam), 1940–
The early prose of William Carlos Williams, 1917–1925.

(Harvard dissertations in American and English
literature)
Originally presented as the author's thesis (Ph.D. —
Harvard University, Cambridge, Mass., 1971).
Bibliography: p.
1. Williams, William Carlos, 1883–1963 — Prose.
2. Williams, William Carlos, 1883–1963 — Aesthetics.
3. Poetry. I. Title. II. Series.
PS3545.I544Z66 1987   818'.5208   87-13162
ISBN 0-8240-0066-8

*The volumes in this series are printed on
acid-free, 250-year-life paper.*

Printed in the United States of America

The Early Prose of William Carlos Williams: 1917-1925

A thesis presented

by

Geoffrey Hallam Movius

to

The Department of English

in partial fulfillment of the requirements

for the degree of

Doctor of Philosophy

in the subject of

English Literature

Harvard University

Cambridge, Massachusetts

January, 1971

Contents

Introduction   i

I.   Prose before <u>Kora</u> <u>in</u> <u>Hell</u> (1917-20)   1

II.   <u>Kora</u> <u>in</u> <u>Hell</u>:   <u>Improvisations</u> (1920)   16

     The Prologue   16

     The Improvisations   32

III. <u>Contact</u> (1920-23):   Essays and Editorials   55

IV.   <u>The</u> <u>Great</u> <u>American</u> <u>Novel</u> (1923)   72

V.   The Prose of <u>Spring</u> <u>and</u> <u>All</u> (1923)   88

VI.   <u>In</u> <u>the</u> <u>American</u> <u>Grain</u> (1925)   110

Footnotes   162

A Selected Bibliography   174

Introduction

The poetry of Williams Carlos Williams is now generally recognized as among the most important and influential written in this country during the twentieth century. He has had a major impact on almost every American poet of stature writing today, and was a personal friend and mentor to many of them.

One area of this man's achievement that has only recently begun to receive the attention it deserves, however, is the prose: essays, stories, novels, plays and prose poetry.[1] It was in his prose that Williams explored at length many of the ideas behind his poetry. The subjects with which the poetry deals are frequently treated more fully, or in a different way, in the essays and fiction. The work of the early years of Williams' career as a prose writer--from 1917 to 1925--is of particular significance, for in it we find clues to the later development of the man and the artist.

The purpose of this dissertation is to examine all of the major and much of the minor non-poetic work of Williams over a crucial developmental period of his art and thought. My aim will be to trace the growth of a mind by discussing the writing in the contexts both of personal experience during those years and of the growth of attitudes which sometimes relate more to the creative act itself than to the life surrounding them.

During these nine years Williams developed most of the approaches to his craft, and the concepts behind these approaches, which tempered his work as a poet and prose writer over his entire life. His intellectual and artistic development were particularly accelerated during the 1920's, partly because of the challenges of a highly provocative and stimulating company of literary friends and enemies and partly because of the exigencies of personal growth. This essay deals principally with those concepts which were of particular concern to Williams throughout an important period of his growth and development as an artist.

I. Prose before <u>Kora in Hell</u> (1917-20)

Between 1909 and 1925, William Carlos Williams became known in literary circles both in this country and abroad as a highly independent writer of talent and originality. To Hart Crane in the fall of 1928 he seemed "perhaps the liveliest man in America."[1] William Rose Benét, on the other hand, simply (though inaccurately) labelled Williams a writer "who first appeared as an Imagist in <u>The Globe</u>, a magazine edited by Alfred Kreymborg in 1914."[2] Benét continued, "He is an original poet of the left wing whose theorizing has frequently hamstrung his inspiration. Nevertheless he has produced some highly original work." Williams himself would probably have been amused by Crane's exuberance and annoyed with Benét's patronizing. But he was certainly both lively and original, and, as this essay will try to make clear, he was also one of America's most prolific and imaginative modern writers.

In 1910--a year after the publication of his first book, <u>Poems</u>--Williams began to practice medicine full time in Rutherford, New Jersey. He was married in December, 1912, two months after publishing seven new poems in Harold Monro's London magazine, <u>The Poetry Journal</u>. Williams' old college friend, Ezra Pound, had secured their publication and himself contributed an "Introductory Note."[3] In 1913 Williams' first son, William Eric, was born, followed three years later by his second, Paul. During this time Williams was building his practice in Rutherford and travelling frequently to New York City both for clinical work and for literary gatherings. Through the latter he became especially friendly with Alfred Kreymborg and those associated with the magazine Kreymborg edited, <u>Others</u>.

In 1917 came another book of poems, Al Que Quiere!, printed this time in Boston by the Four Seas Co., at some personal expense to the poet himself.[4] It was also in 1917 that Williams began to appear regularly in print as a prose artist and essayist. He had had one lengthy letter to Harriet Shaw Weaver about Others published in The Egoist in the preceding year;[5] but his two-part criticism of Dora Marsden's "Lingual Psychology" which appeared in the same magazine in April and August of 1917 was his first major essayistic venture.[6]

In the first part of the review Williams agrees with much of the spirit behind Marsden's analysis of the history of man's development in terms of the "male" and "female" psyches. He deplores with her the traditional domination of the female by the male and looks to a new era. But he ends with the real reason for his taking issue with her: "For me . . . the edge of all Miss Marsden says lies in a covert attack on the 'creative artist.' For this reason, and being profoundly impressed with the great practical importance of her work, I will take delight in striking back."

The second installment of Williams' evaluation of "Lingual Psychology" is interesting in that it gives the reader a clear idea of Williams' current attitudes toward the sexes and, presumably, his feelings about his own masculinity and its relation to his creativity.

> I think it is fairly safe to say that male
> psyche is characterized by an inability to
> concede reality to fact. This has arisen
> no doubt from the universal lack of attach-
> ment between the male and an objective world
> --to the earth under his feet--since the male,
> aside from his extremely simple sex function,
> is wholly unnecessary to objective life: the
> only life which his sense perceives. He can
> never be even certain that his child is his
> own. From this may arise some of the feeling

> a man has for his mother, for in her at least
> is a connexion with the earth, if only a pas-
> sive one, though even here he cannot be cer-
> tain that his mother is his own, for being
> without the use of mind or senses at his birth
> he can have no direct knowledge of it.
>
> Thus man's only positive connexion with
> the earth is in the fleeting sex function.
> When not in pursuit of the female man has
> absolutely no necessity to exist. But this
> chase can never lead to satisfaction in the
> catch, never to objective satisfaction. . . .
>
> Thus the male pursuit leads only to fur-
> ther pursuit, that is, not toward the earth,
> but away from it--not to concreteness, but
> to further hunting, to star-gazing, to idle-
> ness. On this fundamental basis rests the
> male psyche; it cannot but remain agnostic
> in a concrete world; it is extremely simple.
>
> . . . .
>
> Man will only work when forced to do so, or
> when inveigled into it by a woman, or at least
> by a predominant female psyche. Whatever work
> he does do is not for results, which can mean
> nothing to him, but for the drunkenness there
> is in it. _Soyez ivre!_ If he find not drunk-
> enness in his work it is empty for him. 7

The style here is in some places pedantic, and in others it mutters in

terms too personal to be pertinent, or perhaps even wholly intelligible.

But the fact that he felt called upon to reply at such length to this sec-

tion of Dora Marsden's cloudy "philosophic algebra" indicates more than an

average interest in the relations between the sexes, and a keen desire on

Williams' part to define his own identity and experience adequately in

terms of sexual psychology.

In October, 1917, three prose "improvisations" appeared in The Lit-

tle Review. These were the first of the experimental pieces written dur-

ing the year which were eventually to be collected in Kora in Hell in

1920. Their appearance marked an important departure for Williams, though

their obscurity must have puzzled those who knew his previous work. I

shall treat them in detail in a later chapter, when I discuss the improvisations in Kora.

Also in October a "prose poem," "The Delicacies," was printed in The
Egoist.[8] It has been described as an improvisation, but it is not like anything in Kora in Hell. Williams himself was presumably aware of that fact,
for he omitted it from the book, choosing instead to include it in his
fourth collection of poems, Sour Grapes, in 1921. It is an impressionistic
description of a contemporary suburban dinner party which may be the germ
of a chapter in the much later novel, The Build-up.[9] Because it is essentially descriptive narrative rather than "improvisational," one might well
call it the first of Williams' "sketches" to appear in print.

In November The Poetry Journal published Williams' essay, "America,
Whitman, and the Art of Poetry."[10] In the notes on contributors, Harold
Monro wrote that "this is the first specimen of his prose [to be published
in The Poetry Journal], which is considered by many fully as remarkable
as his poetry," exhibiting a flair for the non-committal observation which
much have amused Williams if he ever bothered to read it. The prose of
this essay alternates between confusing verbosity ("Nothing comes out of
the air, nor do we know whence anything comes but we do know that all we
have receives its value from that which has gone before"); and the clear,
challenging statements of a literary rebel ("let it be stated with finality that 'free verse' is a misnomer").[11] At his best Williams is straightforward in explaining the artistic philosophy of the new movement with
which he identified:

> The only freedom a poet can have is to be
> conscious of his manoevres [sic], (12) to
> recognize whither he is trending, and to

> govern his sensibilities, his mind, his will
> so that it accord delicately with his emo-
> tions. Free verse merely means verse whose
> proper structure escapes a man's efforts to
> control it. And without comprehension there
> will be little unfolding. . . .

He went on to discuss Whitman and to acknowledge for the first time his

sense of Whitman's overpowering domination of modern American poetry.

> Whitman aside from being the foremost analyst
> was above all a colorist--a mood man. He des-
> troyed the forms antiquity decreed him to take
> and use. He started again naked but built not
> very far. What he did do was to color every-
> thing he touched with the hand of a J. W. M.
> Turner. His poems fall apart structurally but
> the sweep of his mood, the splendour of his
> pigment blends his work into some semblance of
> unity without which no work of art can be said
> to exist. . . . We cannot advance until we
> have grasped Whitman and then built on him.
> . . . .
>
> The only way to be like Whitman is to write
> unlike Whitman. 13

It was to take Williams his artistic lifetime fully to respond to this

challenge.

In January, 1918, The Little Review published eighteen more "impro-

visations." In June they printed an essay, "Prose About Love."[14] The es-

say is a warm defense of love and marriage which pokes fun at those who

believe an artist cannot celebrate married love: "marriage, ridiculous-

ly, is the great stumbling block of all commentators on love. . . . Mar-

riage is permanent. And we know of course that love is changing." Wil-

liams offers the Decameron as an ideal celebration of love, pure and sim-

ple, and scoffs at the academic assertion that it represents first and

foremost a satirical attack on the clergy. He finds Boccaccio success-

ful because he "lived at a time when love was at the noon." And he asserts that later celebrants--including Suderman, Wagner, Lope de Vega, Ibsen and Shaw--all fell short of the mark. He writes of marriage that its chief characteristic is "its earthiness, its stability. It argues a certain firmfootedness of the spirit. . . . To a man of spirit the loss of his chosen wife will be a spiritual catastrophe of such magnitude that he cannot envision it without expressing at the same time a sense of insecurity extending down to the foundation of his personal consciousness. . . . Divorce is either a lamentable confession of stupidity or it is ineffective. Shelley made a profound mistake in sharing the popular confusion as to what marriage is and is not." He then supports his claims for married love with a roll-call of great married lovers from the past: "Francesca was married, Guinevere was married, Ysoldt was married, Mellisande was married, Deirdre was married, Helen was married, Beatrice was married and of course Odysseus was married--but men are more secretive about these things than women are, at least they do not let themselves get put into literature." This last shift of mind is typical of Williams at his best. He manages with one brief clause to stop the reader dead in his tracks and move him to another area of the imagination. It is a highly "poetic" device in its economy and effect. At the end of the essay, this technique of shifting the emphasis and meaning of his words is employed once again by Williams in a playful closing remark. "One should not forget of course," he writes, "that manners are not nearly on a level with art. It is pure stupidity to act as if they were--which of course salts all I have said."

In December another short piece, "The Ideal Quarrel," was printed in The Little Review, as well as a prose translation made by Williams and his father of Rafael Arevalo Martinez' "The Man Who Resembled a Horse." [15] The

latter is akin in its surrealism, tone and imaginative power to some of
the improvisations written the previous year. It is a bizarre but slightly sentimental Dadaist description of the narrator's relationship with
"Aretal," a friend who resembles a horse in his movements, postures, and
eventually in his psychological composition. Aretal seems to his friend
part horse, part man, and part sphinx. Colors are especially important in
Martinez' story, as they often are in Williams' improvisations and poetry.
And it is interesting that Williams should have chosen to work on a piece
in which the central character, like many of those in the improvisations,
is related to an animal.

In 1919, The Little Review, a magazine of which Williams grew very
fond and contributed to regularly until its demise in 1929, published more
of his prose. In the February-March issue there were "Three Professional
Studies," which are, like "The Delicacies," not correctly improvisations
but closer to autobiographical fragments or the germs of short stories
about his practice in Rutherford. [16] The first, "The Doctor," is frank to
a painful degree about the author's own inner realities and state of mind,
but it remains almost clinical in its remoteness and objectivity about
highly personal material. He begins:

> My intelligence will not permit itself
> to be insulted. All or nothing and since
> I cannot accept all,--except by proxy,--
> nothing. I stand still. I practice medi-
> cine in a small town. I reserve myself for
> myself. I indulge my intelligence, prefer-
> ring that whisky to another. I read Dora
> Marsden's practical philosophy and smile;
> it calls to my mind an image of J. P. Morgan.
> I am a young man, I am in perfect health,
> I am agile, good looking. I do not smoke
> since it drugs the intelligence; I want all
> my reactions. I do not drink except for the

> taste; I despise the lurid vapors of alcohol.
> I do not care much for illicit relations with
> women. I am married and have two children.
> When my father died last week I saw that the
> funeral was decently done. I was affected by
> the burial service. I felt warm toward my
> mother. I felt grateful to my wife and others
> for their solicitous behavior. . . . I saw
> all details carried out and what--? Joyce's
> talk of the funeral ride was in my head as I
> journeyed to the graveyard behind my poor fa-
> ther's dead body. Joyce's technique seemed
> to me childish--Victrola. 17

I quote at such length from this piece because it seems to me the clear-

est picture available of Williams as he actually saw himself at the time;

and because it offers us in quiet clarity a different personality from

that he reveals elsewhere.[18] Further on, Williams speaks of his aspira-

tions and his technique as a writer who is also a busy young doctor. "I

want to write. It does not drug my senses, it sharpens them. It is the

holy ghost of that trinity: The Senses, Action, Composition. I am damned

only when I cannot write. . . . I go in one house and out of another prac-

ticing my illicit trade of smelling, seeing, hearing, touching, tasting,

weighing. I myself. I have no other profession. . . ."

In the second of the three short studies, "Mrs. M.," and in the last,

"Something," Williams proceeds to demonstrate the technique he described

in "The Doctor." "Mrs. M." is a description of his visit to the home and

bedside of a young woman who has collapsed after getting up one morning.

It is a beautiful piece of sensitive reportage of her well-to-do subur-

ban household, her character and appearance, and of her physical condition

and his own observations on her illness. The story gains in intensity as

Williams examines the woman, noting calmly her excitement at having a

"strange man" touch her intimately. As the doctor probes for symptoms of serious illness, one senses his growing apprehension; and the reader and doctor share a feeling of relief as it emerges that there is nothing finally wrong with the woman that a little slow-down and more attention from her husband will not cure.

"Something," the third piece, involves us with the problems of ministering to the slum poor and conveys Williams' frustration and anger with people too ignorant or poor to help themselves or care for each other. "Stuiso. Morse Avenue. Right away. Something in her throat--come quick. I go. It's the woman herself. She has been ill a week. Damn these people. One look. Peritonsilar abcess, right side."

The woman in this piece is in clear contrast to the middle-class "Mrs. M." Williams operates on her then and there, lancing the infection in her kitchen amidst the unsympathetic members of her family and the general filth. As a doctor, Williams clearly has no great love for these people: they are dirty and uncaring and they can never pay him adequately for his services. But it is among these people, the families of "Guinea Hill" as he called them, that he practiced faithfully for almost fifty years. If one sometimes wonders--quite justifiably--about the motivation behind this lifelong exposure to people and situations that he often found distasteful, irritating or downright repugnant, perhaps the clearest explanation is offered at the end of this last of the three "professional studies." "I want to write, to write, to write. My meat is hard to find," exclaims the young doctor. And he adds a question which hearkens back to the initial disclosure of cowardice that opens these studies and becomes a direct challenge to himself, "What if I have not got the courage?"

In April, The Little Review printed half of the Prologue to Kora in

Hell, entitled "The Return of the Sun." The section ended with the letter from Wallace Stevens. In May The Little Review brought out the second part of the Prologue to Kora and announced the book's future publication by Four Seas. There were other short prose pieces which appeared during the year, and nine more of the Kora improvisations were printed in The Little Review.

Others for April-May, 1919, printed Williams' first published dramatic writing, a one-act play called "The Comic Life of Elia Brobitza."[19] It is an interesting piece of work--though hardly comic--about an old woman whose fantasies on the night of her death provide the actress in her role with the opportunity of playing three distinctly different parts corresponding to different times in the old woman's life. In one of the brief flashbacks, the girl Elia's lover, Flavi, tells her a shortened version of Chaucer's "Reeve's Tale," complete with a "pale drunk" miller. It shows considerable talent at writing for the theater, and in his stage directions, Williams demonstrates that he is thoroughly familiar with the possibilities of stage action.[20]

Williams was most irascible in his shorter or less ambitious essays, usually reviews, appreciations, or responses to criticism, and usually concerning writers or subjects connected with the "new literature." He was increasingly involved in the advocacy or defense of modern art or artists against critics, scholars, and the literary establishment. It is in these years that Williams' reputation as an anti-intellectual and radical flowered; and perhaps it is not surprising that Benét should have thought that his "theorizing . . . frequently hamstrung his inspiration." That is how he must often have appeared to those of the New York or Boston literati who at least knew of his existence or bothered to read his work. A con-

siderable number of them did know of him or read him, however, and more
than one crossed swords with him over real or imagined differences.

The correspondence between Williams and Amy Lowell which took place
during the years from 1916 to 1921 is comprised of sixteen letters in all,
eight from each party.[21] It shows us something of Williams at his most sensitive, his most rebellious, and his most vexatious. The "break" which occurred in 1916 between these two over what Williams felt were Miss Lowell's
efforts to sabotage Others and quash young writers in general is traced
clearly in his letters to her. But it is interesting to note that Amy Lowell
handled Williams gently and dextrously in responding to his considerable
rudeness; and that she went to some lengths to clear herself of his charges
against her and to win his confidence and friendship. In August of 1918,
her poem "Appuldurcombe Park" finally gained her Williams' grudging admiration. She answered his gruff and qualified praise with the gentleness of
an impregnable despot well pleased that the enfant terrible had finally
laid down his arms and come around. She regretted, in her letter dated
August 7, 1918, that Williams had been such "a pesky touchy creature."[22]
"There are not many of us," she concluded, "and some time one might like
to talk to you. Still, I think it might be something like smelling at a
thistle."

The July number of Others (V, No. 6) was its last and a suitably
prickly Williams took over the editing chores from Kreymborg to produce
an issue in honor of Emanuel Carnevali, the young Italian poet and novelist then living in America.[23] The lead editorial entitled "Gloria!" at
once praises Carnevali and condemns the literary ambiance--Others in-
cluded--in which the younger man was forced to exist: "The man is smashed

to pieces by the stupidity of a city of sxxtasxxs," Williams writes. "We older can compose, we seek the seclusion of a style, of a technique, we make replicas of the world we live in and we live in them and not in the world. And THAT is Others. The garbage proved we were alive once, it cannot prove us dead now."

In a second essay in the same issue, "Belly Music," Williams declares war on those critics trying to deal with contemporary American poetry. "I am in the field against the stupidity of the critics writing in this country about poetry today." He also gets off a charge at his old friend Richard Aldington who had written a letter opposing current trends in poetry to The Dial. "Aldington cannot understand that one need not PREFER La Grosse Margot . . . to Heliodora in order to write good poetry. Even in the flare of such a life as Villon's he remains blind so that perhaps after all one has to pardon American editors their taste for loveliness--

> myrrh-tressed Heliodora

bah, bah, bah, bah! I repeat Villon's curt answer:

> Vente, gelle, gresle, j'ai mon pain cuit. 24

"Belly Music" is an interesting essay because it helps us to round out our picture of Williams and to realize what he felt he was up to in these "anti-intellectual" years immediately following the war. One passage shows that he was already pondering Columbus' voyage to America some time before he set the story down as part of In the American Grain in "The Discovery of the Indies."[25] His initial artistic response to the topic is hardly enthusiastic. Rather, he makes it sound as though dealing with historical material is a duty and a chore, certainly not a source of inspiration.

> It is important not to ignore the Coperni-
> can theory, the voyage of Columbus, not be-
> cause these things make a damned bit of dif-
> ference to anyone, especially to a poet, but
> because they stick unconsciously in a man's
> crop and pervert his meaning unless he have
> them sufficiently at his finger tips to be
> ware [sic] of them. And the mark of a great
> poet is the extent to which he is aware of
> his time and NOT, unless I be a fool, the
> weight of loveliness in his meters. And I
> cannot see anything worth striving for save
> greatness.

He goes on to explain his militant attitude toward critics and even his
fellow writers. It is an accurate and unflinching appraisal of his position.

> I MUST demand what I do. I must fight back
> at the stupidity around me. I acknowledge
> inadequacy of information, elliptical state-
> ment, too vague generalizations SOMETIMES.
> I am not always a fair critic. I am a man
> doing that which does not fit his turn of
> mind. I think it is important to state these
> things. A more able scholar, a cooler brain
> with a wider fund of information more acute-
> ly focused--since these things are unenlisted
> in the important matters which concern me I
> write to fill the gap, to emphasize a need
> which I don't know better how to make appar-
> ent.

"The Ideal Quarrel," a short piece mentioned earlier, published in
the December, 1918, Little Review, may also provide some insight into Williams' attitudes toward his peers and toward the old and the new in literature. He is talking of fundamental disagreement between people--per-
haps in marriage--and the ways in which such a schism must move toward
dialectical resolution, "for to break and begin a new alignment is reca-
pitulation but to recement an old and dissolving union is without precedent, a totally new thing. The old union in this case is a part of the

new and being directly a part needs no counterpart, the recemented union being ready at birth to go forward. Every part of a changed alignment is a counterpart of the dead one." He concludes by admonishing the reader, "This is hard but very important." One recalls his remarks on married love and the folly of divorce in the earlier "Prose About Love," and sees here the same determination to perpetuate while rebuilding relationships or institutions without tearing them asunder. The emphasis in "The Ideal Quarrel" is on re-creation, on organic change. Even when emotions are at the flood, their thrust should be toward consolidation and renewal: "Anger will recreate a world. . . . The hard backbite of anger recurring in the ebb flow is sturdiness holding its own."

Whether these pronouncements were intended to be taken at face value or not, or whether they were written in the same hot, compulsive manner in which the improvisations often were--to "get it out"--they nonetheless stand as something of a beacon-light for navigation among Williams' basic thinking at this period, and they chart for us some of his basic intellectual commitments. Despite frequent heated proclamations and skirmishes, his literary radicalism in these early years was one favoring peaceful revolution. His demands and assertions were not the less strident for that; but as in his essay on Whitman, he remained singularly aware of the value of both the old and the new in the creation of a lasting American art in the twentieth century.

In The Little Review for August, 1919, Williams wrote in praise of the poetry of his friend Wallace Gould, the Maine poet, whose work had appeared in Others.[26] The review is at once a defense of Gould's simplicity of style and his localism, and an opportunity for Williams to get off another broadside at the establishment. "Wallace Gould is an exquisite performer upon his instrument," he begins. "By his instrument I mean his Maine." He proceeds to attack Gould's detractors (and by implication his own). "This is the thing that no tissue paper critic can stand. That an artist should be a man of power; that he should use a catbird to proclaim the death of the whole world; that he should be such a mean fellow as to befool the poor critic who has been trying so hard to explain things--." It is admittedly a polemic response, perhaps lacking in objectivity toward his friend's poetry--which Williams subsequently gave rather lukewarm treatment.[27] But throughout his life Williams was never one to shrink from critical controversy. "I differ from some of my companions," he wrote in a later issue of The Little Review, "in that I do not disdain to attack the critic. I do not disdain to soil my hands with death. I find a certain exhilaration in taking the heavy corpse in my arms and fox-trotting with it as far as I am able. It is not easy to dance with a dead thing in the arms."[28] This is a boast, but it is the honorable boast of the embattled warrior. It is also another example of Williams' gift for the bizarre image which is at once an effective device as he makes his point and at the same time lifts the reader into an imaginative world apart from all controversy, cutting the cable between reality and poetry.

II. Kora in Hell: Improvisations (1920)

The Prologue

The prose "improvisations" written during 1917 and ultimately collected as Kora in Hell: Improvisations in 1920 were the most important
writing Williams produced during these years. The first to be published
were the three which open the book, in The Little Review of October, 1917.
In the same number of the magazine was a short essay by Maxwell Bodenheim,
whom Williams termed "an Isaiah of the butterflies" in the Prologue to
Kora.[2] In one of those peculiarly fitting coincidences which dot literary
history, Bodenheim seemed to call for very much the sort of writing in
America that Williams was trying to achieve with the Improvisations.
Bodenheim wrote: "When American writers become thoroughly [decadent],
and are not ashamed to frolic with words, writing in a passionate surge
in which imagination becomes a tipsy priest, marrying words and meaning,
and waltzing arm in arm down the road with them, beauty in American literature will have its inception."[3] It is interesting to note the simi-
larity between Williams' early exhortation to all men to "be drunk" with
their work in his second response to Dora Marsden, and Bodenheim's alco-
holic figure for his vision of the future of American literature. There
is much of the passionate waltzing of the "tipsy priest" in Kora, as there
is throughout the fiction and poetry of this period of Williams' life.
The spirit of the "Danse Russe" is everywhere.

Williams did not include any explanatory notes for the first three
printed improvisations. Nor were there any notes for the subsequent group
in The Little Review the following January. The reason is surely that

he had not yet written these "brief moralistic statement[s] explaining
the text" as he called them in the Autobiography.[4] The last improvisations
to appear before the book came out were in the June, 1919, issue of The
Little Review.[5] These were accompanied by notes, with the format of a line
between improvisation and explanation (or elaboration) which Williams subsequently explained:

> I was groping around to find a way to in-
> clude the interpretations when I came upon
> a book Pound had left in the house, Varie
> Poesie dell' Abate Pietro Metastasio, Venice,
> 1795. I took the method used by the Abbot
> of drawing a line to separate my material.
> First came the Improvisations, those more or
> less incomprehensible statements, then the
> dividing line and, in italics, my interpre-
> tations of the Improvisations. The book was
> broken into chapters, headed by Roman numerals;
> each Improvisation numbered in Arabic. . . .
> The copy above the line represents my day by
> day notations, off the cuff, thoughts put down
> like a diary in a year of my life. The remarks
> below the line are a clarification of the no-
> tation.[6]

He also mentions in the Prologue that he arranged the improvisations "in
groups, somewhat after the A. B. A. formula, that one may support the other, clarifying or enforcing perhaps the other's intention." The last batch
in The Little Review was accompanied by ten notes for other improvisations,
some of which pertained to those which had appeared earlier and some of
which did not. Williams apparently chose to print them as a sort of general explanation of what he was attempting, for he wrote a brief introduction to them which stated that "These notes have been detached from existing improvisations for their explanatory value." But to have printed them
alone without indicating how they related to the other "existing improvisations" can hardly have been terribly helpful to the puzzled reader.

Perhaps he simply wanted to show any potential buyer that the book would
provide at least a modicum of explanation along the way.

Whatever the reasons for this rather erratic publication pattern, the
book itself appeared in September, 1920. "It is the one book I have en-
joyed referring to more than any of the others," Williams said long after-
ward. "It reveals myself to me and perhaps that is why I have kept it to
myself."[7] In his 1957 Prologue to the City Lights edition he wrote, "The
book as soon as it was printed entered a world which I didn't feel I could
betray so that I did not at first want it to be republished. It remained
more or less of a secret document for my own wonder and amusement known
to few others."[8]

Others did read it, though, despite Williams' modest disclaimer, among
them some of the most talented young writers in New York. Marianne Moore,
an old friend, reviewed it in Contact in the summer of 1921 and wrote that
the "book is alive with meaning; in it 'thoughts are trees' and 'leaves
load the branches'. But one who sets out to appraise him has temerity,
since he speaks derisively of the wish of certain of his best friends to
improve his work and, after all, the conflict between the tendency to aesthetic anarchy and the necessity for self-imposed discipline must take
care of itself."[9] Miss Moore also found him "disdainful and complex." Hart
Crane took Kora very much as its author intended it to be taken. He found
the collection "a book for poets alone . . . meaningless to a large extent
to most people, but very suggestive and, to me, stimulating."[10]

Like much of his writing in these years, Kora in Hell is essentially
a Williams manifesto. Although he was modest and secretive about the book
four decades later, his tone in the Prologue, dated September 1, 1918, is

anything but. One finds there that blend of bravado and reticence peculiar
to the private revolution Williams was waging at the time. The Prologue
is primarily aimed at friends and sympathizers: there is little attempt
made to win support. Like Al Que Quiere! three years earlier, it is really addressed "to him who wants it."[11] There is an odd mixture of ironic self-
consciousness, theories of the new art, and literary gossip in the tone
Miss Moore found "disdainful." Kora is a private book, as Williams knew:
but he also desired to "sound off" with it.[12] He sets forth his views on the
current state of literature and on his friends and enemies in the same cut-
tingly frank way in which he examined himself in "The Doctor." Apparently
bits of that frankness had already cut a little close to the nerve in some
quarters, or Williams had thought better of including them, for he deleted
some anecdotal material which had appeared in The Little Review version
from the book, including a story about Pound and Pound's father. As
he moves through contemporary letters and literary figures, he involves
each subject in some way with his own views on poetry and American writing
generally. He is seldom excessively caustic; rather he sounds like a small
boy giving a stranger the low-down on his family's quirks and foibles, without concern for their embarrassment or the stranger's confusion.

The opening of the Prologue, which Williams subtitled "The Return of
the Sun," begins with a fragment of poetry:

> Her voice was like rose-fragrance
>
> waltzing in the wind.
>
> She seemed a shadow, stained with
>
> shadow colors,
>
> Swimming through waves of sunlight . . .

The figure's "shadowy" nature relates her to another female form in Williams' earlier poem, "The Shadow," who is specifically a personification of Spring.[13] But she is also Persephone, or Kora; and she stands for the poet himself.[14] As Williams pointed out later: "I thought of myself as Springtime and I felt I was on my way to Hades (but I didn't go very far). This was what the Improvisations were trying to say."[15] Perhaps this "shadow" is returning to the earth as the sun does after wintering in the darker regions. As Williams wrote in the 1957 Prologue, "March had always been my favorite month, the month of the first robin's songs signaling the return of the sun to these latitudes; I existed through the tough winter months of my profession as a physician only for that."[16] So the "Prologue which is really an Epilogue,"[17] the last part of the book to be written, begins with a celebration of the ascent of Kora, balancing the descending tone and season of the opening improvisations.

There is one other figure in Williams' life, however, who also relates to the lady described in these few lines. This is Williams' mother. He said later that her influence on the earlier years of his development had been extremely strong; and one might add that it went on being strong throughout his adult life.

> I was conscious of my mother's influence all through this time of writing [1913-1917], her ordeal as a woman and a foreigner in this country. I've always held her as a mythical figure, remote from me, detached, looking down on an a- rena in which I happened to live, a fantastic world where she was moving as a more or less pa- thetic figure. Remote, not only because of her Puerto Rican background, but also because of her bewilderment at life in a small town in New Jer- sey after her years in Paris where she had been an art student. Her interest in art became my

> interest in art. I was personifying her, her
> detachment from the world of Rutherford. She
> seemed an heroic figure, a poetic ideal. I
> didn't especially admire her; I was attached
> to her. I had not yet established any sort
> of independent spirit. 18

What Williams says of his mother relates her, too, to the myth of

Springtime banished to Hades; and the opening pages of the Prologue are

a celebration of her. She was the artistic parent, endowed with a qual-
19
ity of the spiritual that never ceased to amaze her son. Her presence at

the outset of the Prologue is distinctly honorific; but it is an essential

and well-deserved honor in Williams' mind, not an ornamental one. She is

a sort of Muse to him, intimately associated with his thinking and writing.

When he tells us the anecdote of her getting lost in Rome because of turn-

ing the wrong way, he is also commenting on his art as a writer. The story

is analogous to his method in the Improvisations, and an indication to his

reader of what it is Williams intends him to experience. In the untamed,

tipsy, associational world of Kora in Hell the straightforward and familiar

often disappear. The words and sense frequently turn "to the left when

[they] should have turned right," as did Mrs. Williams on her never-to-be-

forgotten European trip.

Moreover it is precisely the modern "fear of being lost"--a fear be-

ing explored by many writers, including Eliot in The Waste Land and Pound

in Hugh Selwyn Mauberley--that Williams tries to deal with in these impro-

visations. "What if I do not have the courage?" asks the writer-doctor of

himself in "Three Professional Studies"; but he keeps on going. It is "the

strangeness of every new vista" which interests the author and the reader

of Kora, not the best route among familiar literary landmarks.

Williams observes of his mother that "there has always been a disreputable man of picturesque personality associated with this lady." She has been a "Penelope" to two handymen, "William" and "Tom O'Rourck," and the three of them become Homeric burlesques as she sobers them up repeatedly with hot coffee or strong ammonia. In a sense this lighthearted allusiveness is a hint of Williams' response further on in the Prologue to those like Hilda Doolittle or Wallace Stevens who assert in their letters to him that poetry is "a very sacred thing" or a "damn serious business." The classics can certainly be employed in the new art, but the main concern is the humanity and "home-grown" nature of the work. Allusion for the sake of adornment or elevation of mood was not what Williams sought; he was interested rather in whatever would serve the purpose of communicating his meaning purely and simply. And, as we shall see, he frequently had recourse to classical mythology for that purpose, though he always transposed it onto the local environment of rural New Jersey.

Admittedly, his mother (like the landscape in many of the improvisations that follow) is "an impoverished, ravished Eden," but she is "one indestructible as the imagination itself." She is not a disembodied classical ideal, or a Provençal lady of high degree, but someone considerably more tangible and immediate. She does not participate in Aldington's notion of "beauty" either: "Her meat though more delicate in fibre is of a kind with that of Villon and La Grosse Margot: Vente, gresle, gelle, j'ai mon pain cuit!" Despite her foreign birth--or perhaps because of it--there is a peculiarly "American" toughness about this woman. Like the bol weevil in Carl Sandburg's song, writes her son, she can adapt to any condition or environment and claim, "That'll be ma HOOME!"

It would be difficult to overlook the similarities between his description of the elder Mrs. Williams and the kind of writing that Williams wanted to see more of in America, and that he intended to produce himself. And there is another element in her personality which relates with peculiar appropriateness to Williams' technique as a writer. It is a quality that is unusual and perhaps slightly sinister, some inkling of a connection with darker powers. Though he feels her to be "by nature the most light-hearted thing in the world," he notes the occasional "grotesque turn to her talk, a macabre anecdote concerning some dream, a passionate statement about death, which elevates her mood without marring it, sometimes in a most startling way."

Williams illustrates his mother's talents as a narrator by relating two dialogues between her and himself. One concerns the undertaker's profession and dwells at the end on the embalmer's practice of filling up the mouth of a toothless corpse for appearance's sake. The other "dark turn at the end" of a story has to do with a certain "Mrs. B." "'They told me: "Mrs. Williams, I heard you're going to have Mrs. B [as a boarder]. She is peculiar." She said so herself. Oh no! Once she burnt all her face painting under the sink.'" Even in such a brief encounter as this, the reader has the distinct sense of being off balance, a little lost. He finds himself (at "Oh no!") dealing with an ordering principle with which he is wholly unfamiliar, and he is unable to follow the train of thought at work. At the least he emerges startled by the sudden shifts in tone and emphasis which occur. Williams analyzes this knack of his mother's in these words: "Thus seeing the thing itself without forethought or afterthought but with great intensity of perception my mother loses her bearings

or associates with some disreputable person or translates a dark mood.
She is a creature of great imagination. I might say this is her sole
remaining quality. She is a despoiled, moulted castaway but by this power she still breaks life between her fingers."

This "seeing of the thing itself without forethought or afterthought
but with great intensity of perception," and the losing of one's bearings
that goes with it are unmistakably related to the kind of writing one finds
throughout Kora in Hell. In her review of the book in Contact, mentioned
earlier, Marianne Moore discusses Williams' own style and use of literary
devices in strikingly similar fashion:

> The sharpened faculties which require exact-
> ness, instant satisfaction and an underpinning
> of truth are too abrupt in their activities
> sometimes to follow; but the niceness and ef-
> fect of vigour for which they are responsible
> are never absent from Dr. Williams' work and
> its crisp exterior is one of its great distinc-
> tions. He again reminds one of the French.
> John Burroughs says of the French drivers of
> drays and carts, "They are not content with a
> plain matter-of-fact whip as an English or A-
> merican labourer would be, but it must be a
> finely modeled stalk, with a long tapering lash,
> tipped with the best silk snapper. 20

Raised to the level of the writing in the Improvisations, the sudden changes
in tone and the unusual juxtaposition of words or rhythms employed by his
mother in her conversation become just such "a long tapering lash." And
this is usually armed with what Miss Moore refers to as "the snapper." "In
the following passage," she writes, "the words 'black and peculiar' would
seem to be the snapper": "A mother will love her children most grotesque-
ly. . . . She will be most willing toward that daughter who thwarts her
most and not toward the little kitchen helper. So where one is mother to

any great number of people she will love best perhaps some child whose black
and peculiar hair is an exact replica of that of the figure in Velasquez'
Infanta Maria Theresa or some Italian matron whose largeness of manner takes
in the whole street."[21] One might add that the juxtaposition of the Infanta
and the Italian matron serves to make the lash that much more limber, un-
predictable and effective.

The pages of <u>Kora</u> <u>in</u> <u>Hell</u> are filled with such unusual imagery and
juxtaposition--moments when the reader is suddenly aware of a different
torque driving the language and the thought behind it. Williams frequently takes a direction totally unanticipated, and the reader is taken by sur-
prise, finding himself "lost." But when the writing is at its best, this
technique is not disquieting; rather it is a warm invitation to share "the
strangeness of every new vista." The Prologue itself, in addition to setting forth ideas and opinions in an uncompromising way, is also in a very
real sense a "speaking before" the Improvisations, using in apparently direct discourse the very tec~niques employed in the "tipsy" world of the
material that follows. Thus the Prologue is not merely a manifesto, it is
the traditional choral act of preparation and involvement.

There are many examples of "improvisational" talent in the Prologue,
and some discussion of its value to the arts in general. Williams tells
us that he once asked Walter Arensberg about the cubists who had so stunned
American artists since Marcel DuChamps' "Nude Descending a Staircase" had
burst among them at the Armory Show a few years before.[22] In response to
Williams' question of "What the more modern painters were about," Arensberg
replied that "the only way man differed from every other creation was in
his ability to improvise novelty and, since the pictorial artist was under

discussion, anything in paint that is truly new, truly a fresh creation, is good art."

Williams continues his discussion on the subject of novelty and improvisational ability, and as he does he dots his prose with "snappers." I shall give some brief examples, italicizing the words or phrases which I think, as Williams wrote of his mother, elevate the mood "without marring it, sometimes in a most startling way."

> I would start the collection with a painting
> I have by a little English woman, A. E. Kerr,
> 1906, that in its unearthly gaiety of flowers
> and sobriety of design possesses exactly that
> strange freshness a spring day approaches with-
> out attaining, an expansion of April, a thing
> this poor woman found too costly for her pos-
> session--she could not swallow it as the nig-
> gers do diamonds in the mines.
> . . . .
>
> Together with Mina Loy and a few others Du
> Champs and Arensberg brought out the paper,
> The Blind Man, to which Robert Carlton Brown
> with his vision of suicide by diving from a
> high window of the Singer Building contrib-
> uted a few poems.

It is not only in individual words or phrases, however, that this genius for the poetic leap to new or seemingly unrelated subjects occurs. The entire Prologue is sliced into sections which at first reading do not always go together, and whose relationship becomes clear only when one views the whole through the lens of Williams' central intention in the essay. There is none of the familiar flow from paragraph to paragraph, or from section to section, which a reader might well expect. The subjects are taken up, worked over and discarded in a manner not unrelated to stream-of-consciousness technique in narrative. It is a technique in prose writing that Williams employs repeatedly over the years between 1920 and 1923.

The Prologue is assembled by topic roughly as follows: Williams' mother; modern art and artists; Marianne Moore's and Mina Loy's poetry; Ezra Pound; Hellenism vs. Romanism ("the ferment was always richer in Rome"); H. D.; the new poetry; Wallace Stevens; several of the commentaries to the Improvisations as "weight to my present fragmentary argument"; love and marriage; Alfred Kreymborg; Jepson's evaluation of T. S. Eliot; Eliot himself; Ezra Pound; Wallace Stevens; Maxwell Bodenheim; alcohol and Charles Demuth; and the nature and form of the improvisations which follow.

While there is occasionally a clear connection between one subject and the next, the total structure is something of a hodge-podge. Part of this is due no doubt to the fact that, according to Williams, "it is the first piece of continuous prose I remember writing."[23] But if it seems at times structurally deficient, one must bear in mind the method which is at work in all of Kora--not only in the Improvisations themselves, but in the Prologue and the commentary as well. The Prologue is unabashedly the work of a prose poet: Williams cites Longinus on the Sublime as "the sole precedent" for its broken style, though he admits his precedent is "far-fetched." In one of the explanatory commentaries he includes in the text, though, he points out that "By the brokenness of his composition the poet makes himself master of a certain weapon which he could possess himself of in no other way. The speed of the emotions is sometimes such that thrashing about in a thin exaltation or despair many matters are touched but not held, more often broken by the contact." What Williams is striving after in the Prologue is the effect he produces in his best improvisational writing, "the simultaneous." For if one but substitutes "mind" for "emotions" in the preceding passage, one has a fairly accurate description of the kind of unique and original discursive writing Williams achieves for the first

time in the Prologue.

In "borrowing from the Greek" for the title, and "borrowing from the

Abbot [Pietro Metastasio] for the form on the page," Williams exhibits some

desire to be linked with earlier writers and traditions, as he admits.[24] But

that is his only gesture toward tradition. His differences with other poets

taken up in the Prologue, and his outright attacks on Edgar Jepson and T. S.

Eliot are based on the belief that newness is the essential factor in all

good art, especially poetry.[25]

Prufrock had come to his attention when he was "halfway through the

Prologue," and Williams described his feelings when he had read it as fol-

lows:

> I had a violent feeling that Eliot had be-
> trayed what I believed in. He was looking
> backward; I was looking forward. He was a
> conformist, with wit, learning which I did
> not possess. He knew French, Latin, Arabic,
> god knows what. I was interested in that.
> But I felt he had rejected America and I re-
> fused to be rejected and so my reaction was
> violent. I realized the responsibility I
> must accept. I knew he would influence all
> subsequent American poets and take them out
> of my sphere. I had envisaged a new form
> of poetic composition, a form for the future.
> It was a shock to me that he was so tremen-
> dously successful; my contemporaries flocked
> to him--away from what I wanted. It forced
> me to be successful.[26]

Whether Williams actually conceived of Eliot in 1918 as his principal lit-

erary opponent, or whether he only fully realized this later on, when The

Waste Land "wiped out our world as if an atom bomb had been dropped upon

it,"[27] his treatment of him in the Prologue was bitter. He does not attack

Eliot's craftsmanship save for noting "the inevitable straining after a

rhyme" which he feels vitiates a line from "La Figlia Che Piange," "the
very cleverness with which this straining is covered being a sinister to-
ken in itself." Rather he finds Eliot's poetry, even "the more exquisite
work," a "rehash, repetition in another way of Verlaine, Baudelaire, Maet-
erlinck,--conscious or unconscious,--just as there were Pound's early paraphrases from Yeats and his constant later cribbing from the renaissance,
Provence and the modern French: Men content with the connotations of their
masters." The threat is a very real one to a writer who celebrates "the
new" and rejoices in his own improvisational skill, for "if to do this, if
to be a Whistler at best, in the art of poetry, is to reach the height of
poetic expression then Ezra and Eliot have approached it and tant pis for
the rest of us."

The battle-lines are clearly drawn, but there is no sense of a genuine personal animosity toward Eliot, despite the epithets. At his worst,
Eliot is a "subtle conformist." The critic Jepson, whom Williams calls
"the everlasting Polonius of Kensington, . . . the archbishop of procurers
to a lecherous antiquity," and a "blockheaded grammaticaster," comes in for
the full force of Williams' blast. The important point is that this section of the Prologue which seems so full of anger and bitterness is not an
ad hominem attack on another poet; it is rather a response to a theory of
literature that is incompatible with and threatening to Williams' image
of the American artist as innovator.

It seems wise to look for a central intention in the Prologue, which
is an essay that Williams correctly felt was important, not to mention "the
first thing to show me to be a prose writer." The following passages can
perhaps provide an axis upon which turn all the theorizing, gossip, and

unlooked-for connections we have discussed:

> The imagination goes from one thing to
> another. Given many things of nearly di-
> vergent natures but possessing one-thou-
> sandth part of a quality in common, pro-
> vided that be new, distinguished, these
> things belong in an imaginative category
> and not in a gross natural array. To me
> this is the gist of the whole matter. It
> is easy to fall under the spell of a cer-
> tain mode, especially if it be remote of
> origin, leaving thus certain of its mem-
> bers essential to a reconstruction of its
> significance permanently lost in an impene-
> trable mist of time. But the thing that
> stands eternally in the way of really good
> writing is always one: the virtual impos-
> sibility of lifting to the imagination
> those things which lie under the direct
> scrutiny of the senses, close to the nose.
> It is this difficulty that sets a value on
> all works of art and makes them a necessity.
> The senses witnessing what is immediately
> before them in detail see a finality which
> they cling to in despair, not knowing which
> way to turn. Thus the so-called natural or
> scientific array becomes fixed, the walking
> devil of modern life. He who even nicks the
> solidity of this apparition does a piece of
> work superior to that of Hercules when he
> cleaned the Augean stables.
> . . . .

> It is in the continual and violent re-
> freshing of the idea that love and good
> writing have their security.
> . . . .

> Nothing is good save the new. If a thing
> have novelty it stands intrinsically beside
> every other work of artistic excellence. If
> it have not that, no loveliness or heroic pro-
> portion or grand manner will save it. It will
> not be saved above all by an attenuated intel-
> lectuality.
> . . . .

> The virtue of it all is an opening of the
> doors, though some rooms of course will be

> empty, a break with banality, the continual
> hardening which habit enforces. There is
> nothing left in me but the virtue of curios-
> ity, Demuth puts in. The poet should be for-
> ever at the ship's prow. 30

The major concepts behind Williams' argument in the Prologue are,

then, essentially three: the primacy of the imagination in any work of

art; the necessity of novelty in achieving a work of lasting importance;

and the notion that the poet must seek to move ahead of his contemporaries

in confronting the world, that he must be, in every sense of the word, a

discoverer before he can be a legislator. These ideas were to shape Wil-

liams' thinking over the rest of his artistic career, though it may be ar-

gued that his concept of "the new" had been modified already by the time

of In the American Grain to include the rearrangement of historical fact

in new patterns. Williams seems to have become aware in the early twenties

of a truth expressed by Dr. Johnson in Adventurer 137, that "it is . . .

not necessary, that a man should forbear to write, till he has discovered

some truth unknown before; he may be sufficiently useful, by only diversi-

fying the surface of knowledge, and luring the mind by a new appearance to

a second view."

The Improvisations

At first glance the "spontaneous" improvisations of <u>Kora in Hell</u> seem
opaque, and one can readily sympathize with Pound, not to mention other,
far less gifted readers, who found them difficult to understand.[31] Williams
was trying hard, as he observed, to be at the ship's prow in these pieces.
There is a shimmering, nervous quality about some of the improvisations,
and often the mind must make use of every conceivable associational short-
hand to come up with a meaning. In others the density of subjective material or the obscurity of allusion makes intentions unclear no matter how
hard the "reader of good will" may labor. But in each, one has the strong
if imperfect impression of the particular mood or theme which Williams is
setting down. In each the writer's task is the same: "the lifting to the
imagination those things which lie under the direct scrutiny of the senses,
close to the nose." Sometimes Williams' ability to "nick the solidity" of
what we think we see is less powerful than it needs to be; sometimes he himself seems unable adequately to pierce through the data or to rearrange it
for us so as to present a new perspective.

The subjects of the Improvisations range over the people and events
of Williams' experience, and each memory or observation becomes the basis
of a unique artistic development through the author's own ability to see
"the thing itself without forethought or afterthought but with great intensity of perception." Often the explanatory notes or commentary are as difficult to grasp as the improvisations they supposedly elucidate. Williams'
description of how they were written, however, indicates that they were not
necessarily devised for the sake of clarification. "I read over the impro-

vised bit," he writes in the Autobiography, "and, without thought, or too much of it, I interpreted, with what grew below the line, all that was above. It made an attractive novelty."[32] He also said of their composition that "I used to get very excited; the interpretations had as much importance to me as the statements."[33] The commentary often provides a sort of variation on the theme introduced in the improvisation.

There are several types of improvisations in Kora in Hell. The first kind, which provides the framework of the book as a whole, is concerned chiefly with the central meaning of the myth of Kora, the seasonal passage of time: from summer to autumn, from autumn to winter, and from winter to spring. As the year goes by, it brings to the writer's attention thoughts of aging, death and renewal and these themes are usually present as an undercurrent in the individual improvisations. There is little attempt to be precisely calendrical in Kora, however. Sometimes one entry apparently seems to go with another primarily because it is part of the same general topic or mood. One finds references to months or natural phenomena which are "out of season" in the wintriest parts of the book. It is hard to trace an over-all movement of decline and resurgence running consecutively through the whole, though such a movement does exist as an outline. The tone of the pieces seems to vary as frequently as the writer's daily moods.

Another type of improvisation one finds is apparently unrelated to time or seasonal change. It usually has as its central concern some aspect of the creative effort and often it serves as a model itself of the artistic achievement or discouragement with which it is concerned. These improvisations are perhaps the most interesting to anyone examining the

growth of the writer's mind and the range of his concerns and techniques
as a developing artist.

A third sort of improvisation is a meditative treatment of some object,
person or utterance the writer has come across during his day, or at some
presumably recent time. In these pieces one very often finds the purest
"improvisational" talent at work.

I.1. provides us with a good introduction to the form, aim and method
of the sequence, although it lacks a commentary. Section I was the first
to appear in print, and it was well chosen by Williams to serve as the beginning of such a complicated work. Since it is a short improvisation, I
include it here in toto.

> Fools have big wombs. For the rest?--here
> is pennyroyal if one knows to use it. But
> time is only another liar, so go along the
> wall a little further: if blackberries prove
> bitter there'll be mushrooms, fairy-ring mush-
> rooms, in the grass, sweetest of all fungi.

I.1. is a "late summer" improvisation, but it also serves as a bit
of advice to the reader which illustrates itself. "Fools have big wombs"
implies that one need not be over-fertile nor, perhaps, over-elaborate to
accomplish one's artistic purpose. The great pity, conversely, is that
those who should produce as little as possible often seem the most fecund.
"Pennyroyal" "presumably refers both to the shortness of the improvisation
itself and the value of its contents. It can be taken to mean either a
small offering or a species of mint with medicinal value "if one knows to
use it." The final sentence sounds a note that is of integral importance
to the reader. What Williams seems to be saying in "time is only another
liar" is that it is unwise to ponder for too long over meanings or "value"
in these pieces. One should instead proceed, "go along the wall a little

farther," and try to find something that can be grasped or can be of use
as time slips by. As one proceeds in this fashion, one travels toward a
point where regular responses are left behind and fantasy and new associational possibilities take over. If one discovery--the blackberries, for
example--proves bitter or unripe, not to one's personal taste or of any
particular use at this stage, then the best option is to go on until one
finds something else. In this case and in this season, we are assured of
finding "fairy-ring mushrooms . . . sweetest of all fungi." The mushrooms
are evocative of both real and fantastic worlds. Where they grow the summer grass becomes uncommonly green and luxuriant in a circle. Hence the
name, and hence the connotations here of fantasy and poetry.

The language Williams uses in this improvisation is perfectly simple.
The initial observation and the ensuing images have nothing extraordinary
about them, once one accepts the fact that the first sentence itself is one
of Miss Moore's "snappers." The total effect is to cut the reader loose
from his accustomed frames of reference and prod him toward an area where
he is on his own with his imagination, responding to each image with his
own train of associations. This can be accomplished only if the reader remains open and sensitive to the delicate indications of Williams' writing.
Obviously no two readers follow the same associational routes, nor do they
arrive at the same perception. And Williams was well aware of the fragili-
ty of these improvisations when confronted by the general reader, and of
the difficulty of any two imaginations following the same lines together.
He makes this plain in two of the interpretive sections printed in the Prologue:

II. No. 3. The instability of these improvisations would seem such that they must inevitably crumble under the attention and become
particles of a wind that falters. It would appear to the unready that the fiber of the thing
is a thin jelly. It would be these same fools
who would deny tough cords to the wind because
they cannot split a storm endwise and wrap it
upon spools. The virtue of strength lies not
in the grossness of the fiber but in the fiber
itself. Thus a poem is tough by no quality it
borrows from a logical recital of events nor
from the events themselves but solely from that
attenuated power which draws perhaps many broken things into a dance giving them thus a full
being.

* * It is seldom that anything but the most
elementary communications can be exchanged one
with another. There are in reality only two
or three reasons generally accepted as the causes
of action. No matter what the motive it will
seldom happen that true knowledge of it will be
anything more than vaguely divined by some one
person, some half a person whose intimacy has
perhaps been cultivated over the whole of a lifetime. We live in bags. This is due to the gross
fiber of all action. By action itself almost
nothing can be imparted. The world of action is
a world of stones.

There is here none of that tone Marianne Moore found "disdainful" in her

review, only the poet's distrust of the "real" world of men. Reality in-

sists upon causes and effects, and on the tangible. Williams is far more

concerned with drawing "many broken things," or things which we imagine to

be broken but which may in fact be connected, "into a dance giving them

thus a full being." This is no more disdainful or outlandish a purpose

than any poet has ever had. Williams, like most serious writers, is aware

that his meaning will only be "vaguely divined," even by one with whom he

is on intimate terms. But by the strength of his art and the summer fer-

tility of his imagination he produces fairy-rings where there were bitter berries, urging the reader always to participate with an open mind and to profit from these short excursions.

I.2. deals meditatively with a specific event, in this case with "Jacob Louslinger . . . deathling,--found lying in the weeds 'up there by the cemetary'." The very name gives this man an identity for the reader, even before Williams goes on to describe him: "white haired, stinking, dirty bearded, cross eyed, stammer tongued, broken voiced, bent backed, ball kneed, cave bellied, mucous faced." By this Chaucerian attention to the man's physical appearance, Williams brings his "disreputable" personality and life clearly across to the reader. Louslinger's corpse looks to one observer "'as if he'd been bumming around the meadows for a couple of weeks.'" Then the writer begins to set his composition dancing as he seeks out the "full being" of this man's life and the death that has come to him. "Shoes twisted into incredible lilies: out at the toes, heels, tops, sides, soles. Meadow flower! ha, mallo-! at last I have you." Three "searches" seem to end with this last triumphant cry. Louslinger finds a meadow flower in his torn and disjointed existence and embraces it with Lear-like exclamations; Death "finds" Louslinger and claims him for its own; and--perhaps an unconscious intent behind the outburst--the artist himself has discovered an image which will free the poetic significance of Louslinger from the fact of his death and enable the improvisation to build upon the event. If one looks for a "snapper" here, it has to be "incredible lilies"--the figure for Louslinger's shoes. From this point everything becomes possible in the improvisation. As the piece develops and the pacing accelerates we seem to enter the old man's confused mind: "(Rot dead marigolds--an acre at a time! Gold, are you?) Ha, clouds will touch world's edge and the great pink mallow stand singly in the wet, topping reeds and--a closet full of clothes and good shoes and my-thirty-year's-master's-daughter's two cows for me to care for and a winter room with a fire in it--."

Finally the voice of the writer returns and merges with Louslinger's rambling fantasy. He yearns for something of the man's barbarous freedom just as the dead man's voice yearned for the security of "a winter room with a fire in it." "I would rather feed pigs in Moonachie," proclaims this defiant voice, "and chew calamus root and break crab's claws at an open fire: age's lust loose!" Liberated by the intoxicant of the very language he is using, the poet here expresses a desire for release from his daily routines. It is the first expression in Kora of Williams' lasting identification with the savage existence of the disenfranchised or the "uncivilized," an identification which was to find its clearest expression in In the American Grain several years later.

In I.3. another experience--this time possibly a remark heard during the day--serves to evoke a brilliantly imaginative response from Williams. Probably his trip to Europe in 1909-10, during which he passed through Holland on his way from Leipzig to visit Pound in London, added material from memory for this piece.[35] But the basic perception on which he builds here is a universal enough one: that beneath "the whitest aprons" and behind "the brightest doorknobs in Christendom" exist the same dark possibilities for fantasy or human behavior. "Housemaids are wishes," and we must assume that Williams believed those wishes to be part of general human experience. "Gleaming doorknobs and scrubbed entries" have as much potential sexuality about them as the "dark canals" that whistle at night "for who will cross to the other side." Once that point is made, once scrubbing and soliciting

are granted to be two sides of the same coin--day and night--through the
equation of housemaids and unmentionable wishes, the possibilities are end-
less.

Williams chooses to pit a "late loiterer" as he says in his commentar-
y, against "an old woman with a girl on her arm."[36] He enters the loiterer's
mind, perhaps from his own memories of his lonely year in Europe, expressing his confusion and self-consciousness as he is offered a young girl
for his pleasure by an old hag who may be her mother. "If I remain . . .
leaning upon my lamppost--why--I bring curses to a hag's lips." But the
writer's--or the loiterer's--mind is also making a leap to the young girl's
thoughts at that same moment. She "knows better than I can tell you" that
it is better to swallow her fear and embarrassment and solicit a stranger
than to be beaten later by her companion.

Perhaps the suspicion that his reader would have to know something
of Amsterdam to read this improvisation with full understanding elicited
the commentary which follows it; certainly this is a straightforward enough
setting of the scene. The magic of the piece itself, though, is in Williams'
smooth progression from the initial anonymous comment, perhaps from a European woman visiting America, that "No woman wants to bother with children in this country," through the connection of housemaids with sexual objects, to the moment of the canal-side when the three figures confront each
other with their dark business. It is worth noting also that that confrontation and the fleeting exploration of the young girl's mind provide a coun-
ter-charge to the opening assertion. Even in spotless Amsterdam, there are
those who are hard at the work of raping the innocent and prostituting the
pure, let alone "bothering" with their children.

IV. 1. is a complicated double improvisation. The first segment deals with the writer's yearning for the return of "Mamselle Day." In the context of the myth of Persephone or Kora, this section may refer to the gradual withdrawal of daylight or of the summer season from the earth. But more immediately it is a plea for the return of a day Williams has just lived through, and for the past which, as he points out in the commentary, is "past forever." He intensifies the yearning by personifying the day, identifying it with a woman wearing "little shell ornaments so deftly fastened," perhaps someone he has actually seen and been attracted to. The very streets have come alive in this night of the writer's loneliness to "smile with shut eyes," in a kind of unconscious mocking denial of his plea. He has even gone so far as to consult the moon "twice . . . since supper," in his imagination--or possibly on walks he has taken, but it has provided no solution. Williams ends by promising "to be wiser this time" if the past--as day or as woman--will only give him another opportunity. The commentary provides advice to the forlorn and wistful by urging them to take some measure of joy in the fact that "by virtue of sadness and regret we are enabled to partake to some small degree of those pleasures we have missed or lost but which others more fortunate than we are in the act of enjoying." It is wise counsel, but it does not seem to provide real relief; it is an afterthought, not an interpretation.

In the second segment of IV. 1. we are provided with a description and an example of the writer at the most difficult of all tasks, the act of creating something out of a void. He is fully aware that if he were to be seen in the frenzy and despair of his writing--"in this state!"--then the traditional "wings" of poetry or song "would go at a bargain." He expresses

the goal of every artist, the power "to hold the world in the hand"; but
he suddenly breaks off, having discovered that even as he embarks on the
creative act, he has come upon "a brutal jumble." Every technique he employs to improve his condition--"by direct onslaught," as he indicates in
the commentary--produces an unsatisfactory result. If real or psychological "stones" are moved then "ants scurry," taking with them their most
precious possessions, the eggs of their queen. It is possible that Williams
is referring to the elusiveness of material for his improvising at this
point, certainly the frustration of the "brutal jumble" would seem to support this interpretation. But he is also demonstrating in this piece the
necessity of striving again and again "with renewed vigor," even in the face
of perpetual disappointment. Behind the struggles of the ants themselves,
as behind the striving of Sisyphus, lies the final goal of all human activ-
ity--to achieve something lasting. This is "the obsession of the gifted."
As Cezanne worked on for at least twenty years without critical acclaim,
indeed with considerable critical abuse, it is necessary for the writer to
"burrow, burrow, burrow" in the continuing belief that "there's sky that
way too if the pit's deep enough." Such a simple belief is based on the
child's or the primitive's observation of Nature, or so I take the mention
of the stars' authority to mean. Possibly the sparkling of minerals in the
earth is also involved. But it is worth remembering here Dante's emergence
from another "brutal jumble," the Inferno:

> salimmo suso, ei primo ed io secundo
>
> tanto ch'io vidi delle cose belle
>
> che porta il ciel, per un pertugio tondo;
>
> e quindi uscimmo a riveder le stelle. [37]

This improvisation is essentially autodidactic in intent. Faced with the despair of confusion, sterility, or lack of recognition, the artist has two options open to him. He may either stop work or continue on and produce something--anything. In this case what Williams produces is an emblem of the self-curative process of continuing. It is an interesting piece because, like many of Donne's Devotions, it is at once intensely personal and of universal application. Possibly Williams placed it together with "Mamselle Day" because in each the artist has been abandoned. In the first improvisation he pleads for the return of the object of his interest or inspiration, promising to "be wiser" if his request is granted. He sounds in his pleading somewhat ineffectual, and he is apparently ignored, as indeed in the natural course of things he must be. In the second section, however, he actively pursues a disintegrating moment and succeeds in gaining something in the way of a second chance at it. He is able to set down the process of its capture in words by means of the very words themselves.

When Williams writes in the commentary to this piece that "since the imagination is nothing, nothing will come of it," he is not denying or dismissing the very means by which he achieved his art in the Improvisations. Rather he is counselling himself and anyone who cares to listen that the acts of pure imagination taken alone are not enough to produce art or achieve fame. The way to win recognition as an artist, he implies in the commentary, is not to despair and consider oneself the "helot of Fortune," but to "burrow" constantly, adding artistic vigor and order to the imaginative process. To do this is to move, as Williams does here, from despair to deliverance.

Much later in life, Williams singled out V.1. for inclusion in I Wanted to <u>Write</u> a <u>Poem</u> because it was one of his wife's favorites. The piece is

distinguished most by its exquisite opening lines: "Beautiful white corpse

of night actually! So the north-west winds of death are mountain sweet

after all! All the troubled stars are put to bed now. . . ." V.1. may

be related to the improvisation immediately preceding it, IV.3., which al-

so deals with a man's murder and the death of "a young woman who had ex-

celled at intellectual pursuits--," the two yoked forever "side by side"

by the writer because they died in the same night. But it is not essen-

tial that there be any relationship established, any more than the mention

of doorknobs in I.3. and II.1. need imply some special connection there.

"Three bullets from wife's hand none kindlier: in the crown, in

the nape and one lower: three starlike holes among a million pocky pores

and the moon of your mouth" are responsible for the corpse and the autop-

sy being performed on it. Williams incorporates an almost unearthly beau-

ty into this macabre setting. The opening lines achieve the "release" from

reality required of the improvisation, so that from the outset we are in-

volved in a scene which demands our fullest imaginative attention. We are

at least partly in the dead man's mind, seeing things and sensing them as

he might if he were anesthetized instead of dead. As to one under ether,

all lights and the constellation of wounds seem to melt into "this one

good white light over the inquest table." While it wavers between clarity

and confusion, the drugged mind notices the least detail: that there are

two moths instead of the "traditional" one beating their wings against the

light. The motions of the county physician's scalpel seem like "caresses

. . . a little clumsy perhaps--<u>mais</u>--!" The words waver from fantasy to

reality and back in this semi-conscious state. "The Prosecuting Attorney" and "Peter Valuzzi" are quite specifically present; and then there are "the others, waving green arms of maples to the tinkling of the earliest ragpicker's bells." Sight, sound and one's sense of one's surroundings are blended together in this extraordinary image by Williams' technique of drawing what is occurring outside the room into it for a brief instant. Beyond this there are only vaguely perceived disembodied presences indicated by the "kindly stupid hands, kindly coarse voices, infinitely soothing, infinitely detached, infinitely beside the question, restfully babbling of how, where, why." As the night ends so does this fantasia. The autopsy and with it the opportunity for Williams to identify with the dead man are over. To the corpse, the writer and the night itself "the green edge of yesterday," all that is past, "has said all it could."

The commentary to V.1. rings with a kind of finality of utterance worthy of a great sage. The basic instruction it gives is not perhaps so closely related to the improvisation itself as in other cases in Kora. Rather it is related tangentially, by the theme of the passing of all things and the fact that beside death, any word or action is indeed "infinitely beside the point." To be remorseful, writes Williams, in a bit of sound psychiatric counsel, is quite useless. To regret the life of a man, or his death, is "to attempt to fit the emotions of a certain state to a preceding state to which they are in no way related."

Perhaps there is a connection between this commentary and the death of Williams' own father, which occurred on December 25, 1918, after the writing of the improvisation and probably before the commentary was undertaken. [40] The guilt and remorse he felt about the occasion are plain in the Autobiography:

>   Christmas morning, 1918, he had all his
> gifts for the family laid out, each in its
> place, and labeled. The one for me was a
> small cubical bronze bell, as a handle for
> which he had had fitted, the support welded
> in, the ivory figure of an old Chinese phi-
> losopher. Himself? Mother woke and they
> spoke to each other. She fell asleep again.
> At seven she arose. He remained apparently
> sleeping. He was almost finished.
>   She called me, and I went up from Nine
> Ridge Road as fast as I could. It must have
> been a cerebral accident, perhaps from my
> attempts to relieve him the day before [by
> a particularly painful enema].
>   "He's gone," I said. But he shook his
> head slowly from side to side. It was the
> last thing I could ever say in my father's
> presence and it was disastrous. 41

The Confucian tone of the interpretive section is itself peculiarly ap-

propriate when one recalls that last Christmas gift Williams received from

his father.

One of Williams' most beautiful and most moving improvisations is

VII.1. It is chiefly concerned with the seasonal passage of time, in this

case the downward curve toward winter. The piece begins with a short des-

cription of the end of summer: "It is still warm enough to slip from the

weeds into the lake's edge, your clothes blushing in the grass and three

small boys grinning behind the derelict hearth's side." There is a tone

of reassurance here, almost of idyll. But the innocence of the three boys

is overshadowed by the "derelict hearth" behind which they hide to peep

at the bathers. The sense of time passing and leaving ruin behind it is

reinforced by the ensuing realization that summer has left the lakeside,

as has the sun as it sets behind a mountain, further to the south each

day. Summer's light and heat are still present, but now they are "up a-

mong the huckleberries near the path's end and snakes' eggs lie curling
in the sun on the lonely summit." The "path's end," the curling up and
drying out of the once fertile eggs, and the loneliness of the summit all
develop the sense of loss and of chances missed as the season passes. The
narrator is half inclined to brush off his growing sadness, but it seems
to stay with him and to become more personal. "Well—let's wish it were
higher   after all these years staring at it   deplore the paunched clouds
glimpse the sky's thin counter-crest and plunge into the gulch." The
"paunched clouds" and "the sky's thin counter-crest" seem to reflect Williams' growing awareness of his own physical aging, of his own impending
"plunge into the gulch" of time. There is a hint of tumultuous emotions
beneath an apparently controlled and ordered surface in the "sticky cob-
webs" which tell us of "feverish midnights"; and perhaps there is also an
expression here of fear of the "midnight" that is to follow. The image
of a rock cracked by careless Nature or man evokes an ironic response,
"(what's a thousand years!)." The tone is perhaps a result of the desire
to dismiss in this hasty aside what is most disturbing. But the dismissal
is not successful and the mood of depression grows. A pine tree is envi-
sioned wound in a "gray-worm's net," suggestive of a shroud. When it is
suddenly imagined, like the worm, to be a lure for a trout, the whole world
of the improvisation, which has up until this moment been quite real if
increasingly darkened, is suddenly hewn apart and becomes pure fantasy.
Reality drops away as the anxiety created by summer's departure and all
that this symbolizes distorts thought. The narrator recovers quickly and
blames the weirdness of his image on the power of the moon.

The final movement of the improvisation carries us over into accep-

tance for the moment of the end of the season and the descent of one's
life into what the commentary calls "a variegated October." [42] Summer and
youth have gone, "down the other side of the mountain," and we must "carry home what we can." But this calming advice contains within it the seed
of another anxiety, as the commentary points out. Once one determines to
forage among the "blandishments" of maturity, a desire to see "if any has
fared better" ensues. "What have you brought off?" is the expression of
this anxiety, but it is only a momentary flaring up as the piece draws to
a quiet and peaceful close. The fruits of the season *are* real, and their
discovery is an event which soothes the confused and plaintive mind. "Ah,"
exclaims the searcher, "here are thimbleberries."

"The little Polish Father of Kingsland," Improvisation VII.2., is
perhaps one of the better known in *Kora*. It provides us with a revealing
insight into Williams' attitudes toward the poor among whom he worked so
much of the time and toward others who live "with and upon and among" them.
These "pestilential individuals, priests, school teachers, doctors, com-
mercial agents of one sort or another . . . though they themselves are
full of graceful perfections, nevertheless contrive to be so complacent
of their lot, floating as they are with the depth of the sea beneath them,
as to be worthy only of amused contempt." This improvisation, though it
at times sounds prejudiced and myopic, shows us the impatience of a genu-
inely concerned and deeply thoughtful man with those, like the Polish
priest or the school teacher, "Miss Ball," who cannot fathom the "exquisite differences never to be resolved" that are continuously encountered
in the ghettoes.

The little Polish Father's Catholicism, Williams says, is "the way of the music," and the priest is himself capable of the "clear middle A touched by a master--but he cannot understand." The baptism of "a dying newborn" may or may not have real meaning or value. That is not what Williams is concerned with here. What he goes after is the apparently mechanical nature of the act, from the point of view of one whose professional life is given over to bringing children into the world and keeping them alive. His frustration and contempt is closely related to that which he expresses in his short "professional study," "Something," discussed in my first chapter. The common factor uniting the family in that story and the priest in this is their disregard for the "real" nature and value of human life.

"White haired Miss Ball," the teacher, is guilty of another type of blindness and insensitivity. Her task, like the Polish priest's, is to bring people "more into the way of the music," more into the well-ordered, preplanned scheme of things devised by those who will never understand. She tries, without success, to bring music of her own choosing, "her little melody played with one finger at the noon hour," into the ears and minds of children. However, the school in which she plays is, for all intents and purposes, empty. The children are there, as evidenced by their "heavy breathing," "tight shut lips," and laughter, sometimes "two laughs cracking together, three together sometimes and then a burst of wind lifting the dust again." But Miss Ball's tune is "beyond them all." Their minds are absorbed instead with what Williams calls in his interpretation the "ancient harmonies." The wind and dust of Ozymandias' desert are the real components of this scene. There is no "aspiration" in the voices, only random sounds and an occasional brief response to an unseen stimulus.

Williams' business as a doctor and as a writer is clearly not with that "clear middle A" sung by the little Polish Father; rather it is with those "ancient harmonies" of living and dying that are near the center of all existence, and with the occasional sights and sounds that make up our perception of that existence.

The "Coda" to the three improvisations in section VII is specifically concerned with the end of summer, and it seems to reinforce generally the sense of descent we get in VII.1. and VII.2. The Coda gives an ironic impression of "country life in America": "squalor and filth with a sweet cur nestling in the grimy blankets of your bed and on better roads striplings dreaming of wealth and happiness." As the striplings entertain their Horatio Alger fantasies, however, the "cackling grackle[s] that dartled at the hill's bottom" during the summer, join "their flock and swing with the rest over a broken roof toward Dixie." The components of decay, poverty and ignorance with which Williams has been concerned increasingly merge with the end of summer and end of innocence, as indeed they do in the myth of Kora itself. "Country life in America" is over, whatever it once was, and winter--both meteorological and psychic--is on its way.

The commentary on the Coda is one of those included in the Prologue, and like some of the others printed apart from the material on which they were based, it seems strangely without relation to the improvisation with which it deals. It might be said, in fact, that the only common factor in the two pieces is the presence of birds. Williams may here be trying to underline the idea that the way in which he describes his society in its "squalor and filth," its despair and abandonment, is better than stripping

the world of all poetry just because there is no beauty left. There is
no need to be concerned about what others think of one's writing, for "as
there are many birds which sing and many sorts of poems," there are also
"many sorts of fools" who read one's work.

VIII.3. is another improvisation which blends the concern for time,
as well as elements of the Kora myth, with immediate experiences--"the
local"--of Williams' daily life. He not only localizes mythology here,
he also dismisses the European background which is very much a part of him
and of the American tradition. "Spain's riches and Spain's good blood"--
the yellow and red of leaves on the trees--are no longer relevant aspects
of an American scene and no longer fruitful associations to be made by the
American artist. This is an interesting outburst, for it seems to dismiss
the applicability of Williams' own personal heritage to the setting he is
creating here: his Spanish ancestry cannot be related to the "American-
ness" of his art. "Here yellow and red mean simply autumn," he declares.
And he implies that both artist and reader must forget all the intervening European experience that stands between the inhabitant of the New World
and that world itself. The task Williams requires of his reader is that
he feel for himself a one-to-one correspondence between twentieth-century
rural New Jersey and the settings of classical mythology. There is "a
smell of hemlocks" in this air as there is on the Mediterranean hills Williams wishes to evoke. The resemblance between the neighboring region of
"Parsippany" and the name Persephone brings classical myth closer still.
And in that tiny corner of the local scene, "an oldish man leans talking
to a young woman" in a meeting which can only remind us of Pluto and his
unwilling bride. Not only history, but myth repeats itself as one experi-

ences "the local" at its deepest level.

This improvisation is related to the three of XVI, all of which try to establish a correspondence between ancient Greece and modern America. XVI.1. concerns Hercules again, and the piece is approached, like America herself, "Per le pillole d'Ercole!" It is a lively scene, characteristic of Williams' often boisterous sexuality, without any particular relation to the darker thoughts expressed in the other "classical" or "mythological" improvisations. Hercules is portrayed as "a bare, upstanding fellow whose thighs bulge with a zest for--say, a zest!" He has, as Williams points out in the commentary, more in common with a satyr than with the cleaner of the Augean stables; he ends up pursuing "a white skinned dryad."

The mood of XVI.2. is darker and more serious. Here we are told of "giants in the dirt. The gods, the Greek gods, smothered in filth and ignorance." The event which produced this disillusionment was apparently one which affected Williams sharply, for he wrote a poem about it that was included in Sour Grapes--"To a Friend." As he explains in the commentary to the improvisation, "When they came to question the girl ["Lizzie Anderson" in the poem] before the local judge it was discovered that there were seventeen men more or less involved so that there was nothing to do but declare the child a common bastard and send the girl about her business." The sense of loss and despair in the opening lines, which I have quoted above, is continued in the ensuing sentences. "The race is scattered over the world. Where is its home? Find it if you've the genius." Writing about his own experience in the environment with which he had continual contact, and populating that environment with Homer--in XVI.3.--or the deities of classical mythology is one of the ways Williams found to answer that challenge in the Improvisations.

XV.3. is one of the most beautiful of all the improvisations. It has continuity of development and harmony of tone and content which are sometimes missing in other pieces; and it is full of the dancing movement of Williams' best work. The explanatory note which accompanies it is perhaps the fullest expression of what Williams intends in the individual improvisations and in the book as a whole.

It is April at last, but April with the blight of winter still upon it: "whiffs of dry snow on the polished roadway that, curled by the wind, lie in feathery figures." But April means so many things, it cannot be "hedged" or defined so easily with this single opening image, as the writer points out. There are memories presumably from childhood of "a Scotch lady" who "made her own butter," and baked bread made from home grown rye. There is also the fleetingly remembered experience of jumping in the hay in her barn, followed by a more sombre revelation of how, when her husband "lost his money she kept a boarding house." Even in this April reminiscence, then, there are undertones of decline and decay.

There are other aspects of April to be examined, ones which lead further and further from the simplicity and beauty of the opening toward the innermost turnings of the writer's experience. The sexual longings of youth and middle age are touched on in the figure of "Bertha," a girl whose lips, calves and "other perfections" might all be part of "the story that should [be] written" of April if one "had time to jot it all down." Bertha's beauty, like the appeal of Kora herself, is intimately related to her virginity and the inevitable loss of her innocence, for "All beauty stands upon the edge of the deflowering." This thought elicits some frank

remarks from the writer in an "exchange" with his anonymous reader: "I
confess I wish my wife younger. This is the lewdest thought possible:
it makes mockery of the spirit, say you. Solitary poet who speaks his
mind and has not one fellow in the virtuous world! I wish for youth! I
wish for love--!" This outburst triggers some observations on chastity
whose content and tone are as old as literature. "Ah well, chastity is
a lily of the valley that only a fool would mock. There is no whiter nor
no sweeter flower--but once past, the rankest stink comes from the soothest
petals. Heigh-ya! A crib from our mediaeval friend Shakespeare."

There is undeniably a large amount of self-conscious bravado in this
improvisation. But there is real beauty and a harmonious progression of
associations here as well. Williams' flair for the quick, sharp image to
convey a mood and his talent for aphoristic statement are both well dis-
played, and the explanatory section is one of the most important in the
book. In it Williams spells out for his reader what he is trying to do
in Kora technically and how best one may approach his work. He writes:

> That which is heard from the lips of those
> to whom we are talking in our day's affairs
> mingles also with our imaginations. By this
> chemistry is fabricated a language of the day
> which shifts and reveals its meaning as clouds
> shift and turn in the sky and sometimes send
> down rain or snow or hail. . . . But of old
> poets would translate this hidden language in-
> to a kind of replica of the speech of the world
> with certain distinctions of rhyme and meter
> to show that it was not really that speech.
> Nowadays the elements of that language are set
> down as heard and the imagination of the lis-
> tener and of the poet are left free to mingle
> in the dance. [Italics mine.]

This seems to me to be the fullest explanation offered in Kora of Williams'
technique and intentions in the book.

The underlying assumptions of the _Improvisations_ are best or most economically expressed in two statements from the last group, XXVII. In XXVII.1., Williams writes that "The particular thing, whether it be four divers white powders . . . or say a pencil sharpened at one end, dwarfs the imagination, makes logic a butterfly, offers a finality that sends us spinning through space, a fixity the mind could climb forever, a revolving mountain, a complexity with a surface of glass; the gist of poetry." And in XXVII.2. he adds that "There is no thing that with a twist of the imagination cannot be something else." By starting with that latter belief and presenting his reader with sharply drawn images of particularity from which the imagination may soar, indeed from which it is prodded by the wild music of the writing, Williams achieves in _Kora_ a book that stands alone in American literature. It is obscure and often maddeningly personal or annoyingly self-conscious. But for all its imperfections, it is the first great prose work from this most important American writer, and for us as for him, it is a strong and invigorating starting point.

III. <u>Contact</u> (1920-23): Essays and Editorials

    The "revolution" in American writing which Williams often felt he
was waging singlehandedly in the early years received an opportunity for
its own organ when he and Robert McAlmon founded <u>Contact</u> in 1920. During
the two and a half years of its existence Williams put most of his ener-
gies into the five numbers of this irregularly published magazine. He
wrote critical essays, published his own poetry and stories and those of
his friends, and of anyone else he thought lived up to <u>Contact</u>'s standards.
As the first number stated, <u>Contact</u> was "issued in the conviction that art
which attains is indigenous of experience and relations, and that the artist works to express perceptions rather than to attain standards of achievement: however much information and past art may have served to clarify his
perceptions and sophisticate his comprehensions, they will be no standard
by which his work shall be adjudged."[1] Williams contributed this lead editorial paragraph, and he added "Our only insistances are upon standards
which reality as the artist senses it creates, in contradistinction to
standards of social, moral or scholastic value." The premises upon which
<u>Contact</u> was based, then, were very similar to those Williams had adopted
in the Preface to <u>Kora in Hell</u>, though he was a little less violent in attacking "European" or "sophisticated" literature than he had been. There
is here more of a positive program for reform in writing than had existed
in the earlier work--as though in the laboratory of <u>Kora</u> (including the
Preface), he had found a formula for the results he wished. "Assuming
sufficient insight and intellect to convey feeling valuably, we are interested in the writings of such individuals as are capable of putting a

sense of contact, and of definite personal realization into their work."

An afterword for the first number (December, 1920) entitled "Further Announcement," reassured the writers and readers of Contact concerning its aims: "we do not seek to 'transfer the center of the universe' here. We seek only contact with the local conditions which confront us. We believe that in the perfection of that contact is the beginning not only of the concept of art among us but the key to the technique also.[2]

This set of statements in the first number of Contact seems to be the first place where Williams mentions "the local": it is a term which became cemtral to all his work. The idea may have come direct from John Dewey, as Williams implies elsewhere;[3] but it might originally have come to Williams from Marsden Hartley, with whom he spent considerable time and of whom he was very fond. Hartley's Adventures in the Arts, published in 1921, was a collection of articles, reviews and essays, many of which had appeared earlier in Art and Archaeology, The Seven Arts, The Dial, The Nation, The New Republic, and The Touchstone. Williams knew the book well and was to refer to it in Spring and All several times. It is quite possible that he read such articles as "The Red Man," which appeared first in Art and Archaeology for January, 1920, either as printed there or in manuscript. In "The Red Man," Hartley praises the American Indian for his aesthetic prowess, singling out particularly the buffalo dance of the Teseque Indians of the Southwest.[4] What he says of the Indian dancer is surprisingly close to many of Williams' pronouncements in Kora, Contact and Spring and All about what the direction of American writing should be. "The red man is the one truly indigenous religionist and esthete of America," Hartley writes. "As an aesthetic and symbolic performer, he allows

for the sense of mass and of detail with proper proportion, allows also
for the interval of escape in mood, crediting the value of the pause with
the ability to do its prescribed work for the eye and ear perfectly. . . .
His staging is of the simplest, and therefore, the most natural. . . .
Each man is . . . concerned with the staging of the idea," he continues,
"because it is his own spiritual drama in a state of enaction. . . ."
He warmly defends the Indians' dances against "rumors of official disap-
proval of these rare and invaluable ceremonials," concluding that "it is
our geography that makes us Americans of the present, children. We are
the product of a day. The redman is the product of withered ages." What
Hartley thought about the Indian being at one with his surroundings and
being able perfectly to represent them in his dances is close to what Williams was looking for with the idea of "contact with local conditions"
and the sense of a "definite personal realization" in American writing.
Whether or not he got t   idea from Hartley—though one can be reasonably
certain that he got at least a part of it from him—the codification of
his artistic principles in the first number of Contact was an extremely
important moment in his development.

"A Matisse," written for the second number of Contact (January, 1921),
praises the artist's rendering of a nude woman in a pastoral French setting.[5] Williams was excited by the painting because of its power to convey the immediate surroundings of the artist and his model, and especially because Matisse sees the woman's nudity with a pure and natural eye:
"Bare as was his mind of interest in anything save the fullness of his
knowledge, into which her simple body entered as into the eye of the sun
himself. So he painted her. So she came to America." There is purpose

perhaps in that last sentence quite unrelated to the fact that this is "a woman who had never seen my own poor land." For in the way Matisse had dealt with his subject he had indeed "brought" her to America--toward the "American" art for which Williams was so passionately searching. Matisse had instructed Americans in the value of a simple, straightforward rendering of one's subject. "No man in my country," Williams continues, "has seen a woman naked and painted her as if he knew anything except at night." His attack is against artifice, concealment, and prurience, and against the puritan ethic which he feels has produced the great debilities in American art. These barriers to free expression were to become his favorite targets in all the major prose work of the next several years.

Also in the second number of Contact, Williams closed with a "Comment" on critical response to the magazine's first issue.[6] "In answer to all criticisms we find the first issue of Contact perfect, the first truly representative American magazine of art yet published." The tone is quite different from that of the first editorial; and it is an indication of the aggressive and often abrasive statements Williams was to make in behalf of Contact as he struggled to keep it financed and to increase its circulation.

Williams goes on in the "Comment" to propose St. Francis of Assissi as "patron saint of the United States, because he loved animals. The birds came to him not for wheat but to hear him preach. Even the fish heard him." He wonders how Americans are "to love France. These young men of daring and intelligence move into the arts as naturally as our brood moves through football into business." He also seems to offer an explanation of his choice of Matisse as a subject for his essay printed

in the magazine: "If we are to love or to know France . . . it will be
through the mature expression of these men in whom France has physically
realized herself for better or worse. In their mastery of the art of expression France is expressed." He praises Joyce not for his subject-matter and not just because stream-of-consciousness technique follows "some
unapparent sequence quite apart from the usual syntactical one. That of
course is the power behind all good writing. . . ." What interests Williams in Joyce most here is that he "has removed so many staid encumbrances
that his method comes like [a] stroke of sunlight today. He forces me,
before I can follow him, to separate the words from the printed page, to
take them up into a world where the imagination is at play. . . . It is
the modern world emerging from among the living ancients by paying attention to the immediacy of its own contact; a classical method."[7] This is
exactly what Williams praises about Matisse's picture in his essay, and
it is also close to what he himself strove for in Kora in Hell. His sharp-
est realization about America in comparison with the European countries,
however, is not that it is in open warfare with them artistically, as Williams had implied earlier in his career. Rather he finds that "America
is far behind France or Ireland in an indigenous art," and that "those
who would meet the best in Europe with invention of their own must go down
into the trunk of art. . . ." This "trunk of art" is our own "special
local conditions of thought and circumstance." The business of Contact,
he continues, is to stop artists who are "still too prone to admire and
to copy the very thing which should not be copied, the thing which is
French or Irish alone," and instead "to emphasize the local phase of the
game of writing. . . . Every effort should be made, we feel, to develop

among our serious writers a sense of mutual contact first of all . . . .
To this also we are devoted." The figure of St. Francis preaching to the
animals thus has a special significance beyond its usual devotional one.
The mission, as Williams saw it, was to preach to all from and about their
native situation. It did not matter that "when the service was over each
beast returned to his former habits." What mattered was the emphasis on
maintaining contact with "the local," the controlling phases of a man's
experience from which all his perceptions about himself and his world a-
rise, and by which they continue to be conditioned.

In a letter to the editors of The Freeman published in the issue of
January 19, 1921, (II, 45, p. 449) entitled "What Every Artist Knows,"
Williams took a stand against an article by Harold Stearns which had appeared in The Freeman of December 15, 1920. Stearns saw art as a social
phenomenon and felt that great art occurred only at certain special times
in man's history. The early twentieth century, Stearns felt, was decidedly not one of those periods, and contemporary man would just have to do
without great art. Williams argues in terms of his concepts of "contact"
and "the local" that "art lives when men of a certain sort are in contact
with their environment and then only. This may occur at any time." He
continues in the vein of his earlier attacks on critics, pointing out
that "the thing which the philosopher writing about art never can see, is
that art is the product of a certain sort of living contact that can be
made to live, even for discussion, in no other way; that the so-called
fallow periods are no less possessed in this passionate satisfaction than
any other. In fact, that in regard to it all periods are the same." Syn-
tax aside, this is an interesting defense because it gives us some further

understanding of Williams' often scathing attacks on critics in his letters and elsewhere. Most critics are too prone to play down the artistic
accomplishments of their generation or the one preceding it, as Williams
correctly noted, because they are unsure of what is valuable or lasting.
This attitude is in direct opposition to what Williams rightly saw to be
the real business of the artist. And because he was an artist of passionate concern, he could not forgive the critic his remoteness and pessimism.

Williams felt for many years, certainly through the period covered
by this essay, that there was little point in his or any other artist's
carrying on dialogues with the intellectual establishment. He felt instead that artists had to talk to each other, to establish those points
of mutual interest and contact to which his magazine was dedicated. "A-
merica is especially in need of just such talk today," he wrote to The
Freeman, "talk that tends . . . to quicken the artists themselves into
those public demonstrations of their instincts which we are starving for."
He ended his rebuttal with a final swipe at Stearns, arguing that people
who think the art of their own time, or that "spiritual contact with life,
which art is . . . 'unimportant' . . . are nothing more nor less than
vicious."

In Contact III, Williams responded to charges that he was trying to
start a "school" of writers, and even went so far as to point out that
Contact could not insure "everything written under its influence to be
literature."[8] He reaffirmed the central conviction, perhaps a little more
clearly than before, that "contact always implies a local definition of
effort with a consequent taking on of certain colors or sensual values of
whatever sort are the only realities in writing or, as may be said, the

essential quality in literature." He goes on to round on the critics once
more, though in a more balanced way. And in the process he makes an equation which a Freudian might find extremely interesting:

> There are those who have a taste for words
> and ideas, like the Jews, and who are able
> to appraise them, themselves remaining whol-
> ly detached from the affair. But actually
> these figures too, if they are of any im-
> portance, deal wholly with the real liter-
> ary values defined above ["contact," "lo-
> cal experience," etc.]. It is to say that
> the cooks too may be artists and that they
> are known first by their choice of potatoes. . . .
> [Critics and historians] prove only the ex-
> istence of a structure of sufficient reali-
> ty to bear all the fevers without catastro-
> phe. True historians, they are the infa-
> mous Papas of us all. But what of it? They
> are there and we are here. It is a battle
> arrayed, a battle that must be in the end
> yours. O Youth, yours!"

Williams' epithet for critics and historians, "the infamous Papas of
us all," is one which merits extra attention. We have already mentioned
some of the attributes of his attitude toward his own father in the discussion of Improvisation V.1. in Kora: Williams' sense of guilt at the
death of his father, and his inability to say or do "the right thing" at
the right moment. But in the Autobiography, one of the first things he
says about his father in Chapter Four, "Pop and Mother," is even more to
the point:

> I'll never forget the dream I had a few days
> after he died. . . . I saw him coming down
> a peculiar flight of exposed steps, before
> the dais of Pontius Pilate in some well-known
> painting. But this was in a New York office
> building, Pop's office. He was bareheaded
> and had some business letters in his hand on
> which he was concentrating as he descended.
> I noticed him and with joy cried out, "Pop!
> So, you're not dead!" But he only looked up

> at me over his right shoulder and commented
> severely, "You know all that poetry you're
> writing. Well, it's no good." I was left
> speechless and woke trembling. I have never
> dreamed of him since.

If this is not the sole cause of Williams' peculiar linking of critics and literary historians with "infamous Papas," then it is certainly one component in the connection. Williams' almost obsessive distrust of critics is a factor often cited by those detractors who branded him an "anti-intellectual." We have seen, in the discussion of the Prologue to Kora, why, initially at least, he lashed out so severely at Eliot--and that conflict is perhaps not so clearly related to his feelings for his father as this. But it should be pointed out that Williams' father was an Englishman, one whose literary interests ranged from The Origin of Species to the poems of Paul Laurence Dunbar and from Shakespeare to Arevalo.[9] It could be argued that it was as much his father's "presence" and the burden of a preceding tired generation which Williams fought against as a poet and writer as anything else, and that is quite probably as it should be. Williams' relationship with his mother was one reason, as I have tried to show in my discussion of the Prologue to Kora in Hell, why his early writing took the form it did. His ambivalence toward his father is certainly equally much a part of his response to literary traditionalists and critics.

Another personal matter was connected with this particular article in Contact III. Robert McAlmon departed suddenly for London in the early spring of 1921 after marrying Winifred "Bryer" Ellerman, the rich, spoiled novelist who had been (and who continued to be after this unfortunate marriage) a very close friend and travelling companion of Hilda

Doolittle. Williams was upset at the marriage and at McAlmon's departure;

his friendship for the younger man had been an extremely intense one. In

a letter to Amy Lowell, Williams expressed some of his sorrow at the loss

of his friend: "Bryher's sudden wedding must have surprised you. I say

nothing of McAlmon. I wish I had the boy back with me and not lost there

abroad, to no good purpose I feel sure. My God, have we not had enough

Pounds and Eliots? The Sacred Wood is full of them and their air rifles.

But perhaps Bob will do better. He will do better only on condition that

he comes back to America soon. I confess that I am heartbroken."[10]

In A Voyage to Pagany (1928), "Dev Evans" is Williams' autobiographical protagonist.[11] In writing about Evans' relationship with "Jack Murry"

(McAlmon), Williams was more detailed about his feelings for his friend.

Interestingly he linked him with his feelings about his father in the

course of the description. In this passage, Evans has just been reunited

with Murry in Paris:

> Never had Evans forgotten the balance of
> spirit, the distinguished attack upon life
> which had charmed him from the moment of their
> first meeting in New York. The firm, thin-
> lipped lower face, jaw slightly thrust out,
> the cold blue eyes, the long, downward point-
> ing, slight-hooked straight nose, the lithe,
> straight athletic build. The whole picture
> was there--almost intact.
> How would it be inside? for they had had
> great plans together for rescuing life from
> the thicket where it is caught in America,
> the constant pounding in the head. They had
> worked hard to get to an expression--and Jack
> had left--to marry.
> That night at 42nd Street when they had
> parted and Evans knew it was all up, tears
> had stood in their eyes. . . . Jack had
> sailed the next day.
> Oh well, that's America, Evans had writ-
> ten down in his mind.

Now here was Jack. . . .

They were no business partners, no members of a cabinet, not even members of a team. How would they get on? How do men ever get on without some business together? Brothers never do in the same ship, the same regiment-- maybe. . . . The order kills it all. But, as Walsh said, you can't even get drunk with a guy any more without having the name pasted on you.

Evans thought of his English father. How the devil do you love a man anyway? Either you slop over or fight or else you avoid each other. He had admired his father, in some things; loved him--for a few things. But here in Paris, nothing to do--he felt uneasy with Jack.

To hell with what anybody else says, anyway. Evans loved his friend, as some one who brought over to him a section of life where he was weak to get at it, too shy, superstitious, too stately reverential.

. . . .

God bless Jack, he had said to himself a thousand times, I love him. I stand for him.

For Williams to lose such a friend and partner to a woman of questionable intentions and sexual tastes at a time when Contact was struggling hard to stay afloat must have been a great blow . . . but above all to lose him to Europe! The essay "Yours, O Youth" might well be read as Williams' departing instructions to his younger friend.

Not that Americans today can be anything less than citizens of the world; but being inclined to run off to London and Paris it is inexplicable that in every case they have forgotten or not known that the experience of native local contacts, which they take with them, is the only thing that can give that differentiated quality of presentation to their work which at first enriches their new sphere and later alone might carry them far as creative artists in the continental hurly-burly. Pound ran to Europe in a hurry. It is understandable. But he had not sufficient ground to stand on for more than

perhaps two years. He stayed fifteen. Re-
reading his first book of poems it is easy
to see why he was successful. It was the
naive warmth of the wilderness--no matter how
presented. But in the end they played Wil-
son with him.
Unfortunately for the arts here, intelligence and training have nearly always forced
a man out of the country. Cut off from the
dominant [influence] of their early established
sensory backgrounds these expatriates go a
typical and but slightly variable course there-
after.
The few among us who might write well in
any generation, however they will be trained,
fear to believe that in writing it will be
exactly as it has been in other spheres of
inventive activity, that the project has not
grown until precedent has been rendered sec-
ondary to necessity or completely ignored.
It has been by paying naked attention first
to the thing itself that American plumbing,
American shoes, American bridges, indexing
systems, locomotives, printing presses, city
buildings, farm implements and a thousand other things have become notable in the world.
Yet we are timid in believing that in the arts
discovery and invention will take the same
course. And there is no reason why they should
unless our writers have the inventive intelligence of our engineers and cobblers.

Williams was to try to run this "inventive intelligence" to earth as an

artist, to define and symbolize it for the rest of his life. His major

prose works of the next few years--The Great American Novel and Spring

and All in 1923 and In the American Grain in 1925--were devoted to that

end above all else.

After McAlmon's sudden departure, Williams took on Contact by him-

self, getting out one more number in the summer of 1921 and a fifth and

last in June, 1923. "Sample Critical Statement" in the fourth Contact

continues to develop the concept of the local as a key to successful A-

merican writing. Williams again implies that Europe is currently in a stronger position in the arts than America, but he points out that the American writer is in a unique position to overtake his European counterpart: "In exploiting his position in America the artist, aware of the universal physical laws of his craft, will however take off only from the sensual accidents of his immediate contacts. This achievement of a locus, Contact has maintained, is the one thing which will put his work on a comparable basis with the best work created abroad."

By chance the year The Waste Land first appeared, 1922, was a comparatively dry one for Williams' prose, measured by the amount he published. But he was at work on three new books, The Great American Novel, Spring and All and In the American Grain. He was also, as was the case throughout this period, publishing a considerable quantity of verse--by any standards--in Poetry, The Dial (which published The Waste Land as well), Broom and others.[13]

The first three months of 1923 saw the publication of the opening chapters of In the American Grain, though Williams reworked one of them, "The Discovery of the Indies," fairly extensively in 1923 and 1924 before final publication. In June of 1923 the last issue of Contact appeared and in it there were two comments from its weary and somewhat depressed editor. In the first, entitled "Glorious Weather," Williams makes three assertions about writing from which he launches out on an impressionistic, improvisational "ramble."[14] The statements reflect the thinking of a man who is not only ready for but insisting on new departures in art:

   1. The object of writing is to celebrate the
      triumph of sense.

   2. In writing, as in art generally, sense is
      in the form.

> 3. Forms grow rapidly obsolete and must be
> replaced, but the intelligence, the mo-
> tive power behind all composition, seeks
> further for a liberation of pure forms.
> Everything in the development and present
> make-up of the art of writing has resulted
> from a desire on the part of writers to
> clarify the implications of pure form.

Thus writing, for Williams, like painting and music, has come to a new

beginning, a new field of action where "form" is the chief concern. In

this editorial Williams turns away from his preoccupation with "contact"

and "local experience" for a moment to evaluate in a new way what it means

to be an American writer in the twentieth century. It may be that the tone

of his thinking reflects a man still reeling under the impact of that "sar-
15
donic bullet," Eliot's Waste Land, for he ends his piece with a deeply

ironic comment on a notice that "THE NEW PEARSON'S, in the current issue,

heralds the most noteworthy event in the world of letters for the new year

with the forthcoming $1500 Literary Prize Contest. . . ." "Je meurs de

soif," writes Williams, an inhabitant now of his own waste land, "auprès

de la fontaine."

In the closing "Critical Note" on the last two pages of Contact V,

Williams again expresses his bitterness and also his uncertainty about

the direction in which his art--and writing generally--is trending. But

he praises the glorious functional and esthetic simplicity of an African

surf paddle he has seen. And he tells an anecdote about a school play

he attended at which the wrong actress was given flowers after the curtain.

The paddle has the same pureness and practical beauty that Marsden Hartley

praised in the dancing of the American Indian. The incident of the flow-

ers packs the kind of "local" emotional charge for the participants that

has a lasting effect on those involved. In these two examples, Williams
almost seems to be pointing a way for his own writing to follow: simplicity of design, coupled with the sympathetic evocation of powerful feelings,
are certainly the ultimate achievement of his later short stories and many
of the best poems. But whether he fully realized that he was already indicating a direction to take is unclear. The closing paragraph of this
final essay in Contact is deeply pessismistic:

> What is poetry? What shall I say? What is
> their worth, these six poems in this issue
> (one of which was his own "New England")
> judged absolutely--what? beside the cut of
> a West Coast nigger's surf paddle or roses
> to the wrong girl in a play--after the orig-
> inal--that never was original anyway--once
> > Men like birds,
> elaborate kites, descend
> into place;
>
> _____
>
>   - cutting through
> Became a symbol. I had lost the meaning
> Of progression. If I paused, she . . . leaning . . .
> White on the rushes, jade shielding marble,
> No wind blowing, no sound.

Who else prints anything?

The two fragments of poetry here deserve some consideration, marking
as they do the demise of the first Contact. The image of men--or artists--
like "birds" or "elaborate kites" descending "into place" reminds one of
the ill-fated flight of Icarus, and indeed Williams may have felt that
such a precipitous descent had been very much his own experience during
the years of Contact. It is the same descent traced in Kora: a seasonal one that is also related to the reduction of the Greek gods to "giants
in the dirt . . . smothered in filth and ignorance." In such a spiritual
ambiance, Williams seems to say, the artist has been forced into expres-

sions of frustration and impotence. Eliot's poetry and the world-weari-
ness it evokes, are on the rise. "Cutting through," the most important
and significant role of any artist who would express himself truthfully,
has become only "a symbol;" it is no longer actively being done by the
very persons who must do it if art in culture is to survive. When Williams writes that he has "lost the meaning of progression," he is, in a
sense, recognizing the "defeat" represented among other things by the publication and acceptance of The Waste Land, not to mention the simultaneous
demise of Contact. The lady here ". . . leaning . . ." may remind us of
the synaesthetic creature at the opening of the Prologue to Kora in Hell,
Williams' "Muse." She is also, in her simplicity and possible nudity,
reminiscent of the painting by Matisse which Williams praised in Contact
II. But the landscape which was so fully animated with the sights and
sounds of summer elsewhere--when Hercules saw a dryad, "a white flash over
against the oak stems" in Kora XVI.1., for example--is lifeless. The vitality of the female figure seen against the rushes has been frozen into
stone, "jade shielding marble." And the very act of "shielding" the marble skin from view returns us to a Puritan world in which the body must
be concealed. As the voice of the writer pauses, indeed, there is nothing else to be heard, "no wind blowing, no sound." The implication of
the final question is, of course, that no one is printing anything of
value any longer. Others was long since dead and Contact takes its last
breath here.

With the demise of his magazine and wide acceptance of The Waste
Land, Williams seems to have felt the end had come for American writing,
at least for that branch of it he had so vigorously championed. As he

wrote in the <u>Autobiography</u> about <u>The Waste Land</u>: "I knew at once that in certain ways I was most defeated. Eliot had turned his back on the possibility of reviving my world. And being an accomplished craftsman, better skilled in some ways than I could ever hope to be, I had to watch him carry my world off with him, the fool, to the enemy."[16]

IV. The Great American Novel (1923)

During the summer of 1923 William Bird and Robert McAlmon, who was
now living in Paris, brought out The Great American Novel as one in a series called Contact Editions, printed by Bird's Three Mountains Press.[1]
Pound was the editor and the series included his own Indiscretions, or
Une revue de deux mondes, Ford Madox Ford's Women and Men and Hemingway's
in our time, all published in 1923.

The book, very much a product of the Contact years, has been seen as
largely parody and Williams himself thought of it as "a satire on the novel form in which a little (female) Ford car falls more or less in love
with a Mack truck,"[2] and "a travesty on what I considered conventional American writing."[3] But The Great American Novel is full of serious matter.
The basic intention of the book, despite its comic trappings is the same
which lies behind all of Williams' best work: "to learn the essentials
of the American situation." It can be viewed as an attempt to catalogue
the elements which make up the American idiom and experience, and as such
it has much in common with Spring and All and In the American Grain.

The opening is, as Hugh Kenner points out, "a parody of a beginner's
beginning":

The Great
American Novel

CHAPTER I[4]

The Fog.

Humor and parody aside, there are bits of this book which suggest that
Williams is honest enough both to observe and participate freely in the

experience that later novelists like Wolfe and Lockridge took more seriously. He too, after all, as the essays in <u>Contact</u> make clear, was engaged
in a struggle to come to terms with America.

The preoccupation with form which marks the essays in <u>Contact</u> V is
notably present in <u>The Great American Novel</u>. Even the very medium of written expression is scrutinized and found lacking. "Words are not permanent
unless the graphite be scraped up and put in a tube or the ink lifted.
Words progress into the ground. One must begin with words if one is to
write. But what then of smell?" The search for something tangible, something which will convey local experience and personal vision as clearly
as the West African surf paddle or "roses to the wrong girl in a play" is
very much a part of this writing, and it is never wholly to be viewed as
a subject for parody. The primary difference between Williams' consideration of the issues at stake for the writer and the often confused attempts
of others to confront them is that for Williams art does not end in sol-
ipsism. While he participates vividly in the search for a new American
writing--as he does in this book--he is secure enough as an artist to find
the sterile despair and continual self-contemplation of other writers impractical and often amusing:

> There cannot be a novel. Break the words.
> Words are indivisible crystals. One can-
> not break them--Awu tsst grang splith gra
> pragh og bm--Yes, one can break them. One
> can make words. Progress? If I make a word
> I make myself into a word. One big union.
> Such is progress. It is a novel. I begin
> small and make myself into a big splurging
> word: I take life and make it into one big
> blurb. I begin at my childhood. I begin
> at the beginning and make one big--Bah.

Williams was well aware of what Leslie Fiedler calls "the incapacity of

the American novelist to develop; in a compulsive way he returns to a
limited world of experience, usually associated with his childhood, writing the same book over and over again until he lapses into silence or
self-parody."[5]

It is true that the writer pondering his own difficulty, especially
as he begins to write an extended piece, may come to the conclusion that
"There are no words." But Williams' basic premise, however much he may
poke fun at it, is that "if there is progress" then something has been
achieved. The parody itself serves a function for him as he sets out.
It clarifies the pitfalls, dispels his fears, and enables him to keep going. To parody sterility serves the same function as to write seriously
and searchingly about it, as Mallarmé often did: it gets words out and
down. These words may well be "the spin, flare up, rumble, trickle, foam"--
even as they "slowly . . . lose momentum"--but there is forward motion.[6]

As Williams weaves his "travesty" free of its preliminary disorder,
he stitches in a little piece of what Kenner calls "fashionable writing
of the twenties, a notebook exercise" about two men driving home through
the fog from a meeting of the Mosquito Extermination Commission--possibly
a body also related to the treatment of contemporary writing. The passenger lends his handkerchief to the driver so that the moisture may be wiped
off the windshield and then puts it back "wet and dirty" in his pocket.
"But of course the man is a mechanic in a certain sense," writes Williams,
"and doesn't care." "The man" in question was almost certainly Emanuel
Carnevali, who made a visit to the Mosquito Extermination Commission meeting in Hackensack in 1919 with Williams, recorded in the Autobiography.[7]
Both men are, in fact, "mechanics" as writers--and Williams one as a doctor

as well. His sole concern, like that of the driver and his passenger, is
to keep going, using any method and any material available.

When the driver arrives home, he ends up "in his own bed-room with
his wife's head on the pillow in the perfectly clear electric light."
In the opening of Williams' first published short story, "Danse Pseudomacabre," printed in The Little Review in 1920, the doctor's "wife lies
asleep, curled against the pillow."[8] And the blustery, pretentious opening
of the story has not a little in common with the opening of The Great A-
merican Novel: "That which is possible is inevitable. I defend the nor-
mality of every distortion to which the flesh is susceptible, every disease, every amputation. I challenge anyone who thinks to discomfit my
intelligence by limiting the import of what I say to the expounding of a
shallow morbidity, to prove that health alone is inevitable. Until he
can do that his attack upon me will be imbecilic. Allons! Commençons
la danse." In the story a telephone abruptly wakes the doctor out of this
foggy opening and he is summoned to attend a dying child. In the novel,
his wife reads to him from the magazine Vanity Fair until she penetrates
"his mystery" and perceives that as she reads he is not listening but
"stealing" the scene around them "in order to write words." "She smiled
again knowingly. He became furious." This "satire on the novel" is not
limited to poking fun at the work of others; there is a good deal of self-
mockery in it as well.

The second chapter, which lacks a title, opens with the words "I'm
new" and is built around the idea of "progress." Taking a leaf from Hen-
ry Adams, the narrator--who is partly Williams himself and partly a mawk-
ish persona--rivets his attention on the dynamo, "the power house from

which the hum, hmmmmmmmmmmmm--sprang. Electricity has been discovered
for ever. I'm new says the great dynamo. I am progress. I make a word.
Listen! UMMMMMMMMMMMM---." The sound of the dynamo contrasts vividly
with a woman in labor who "with a terrible scream" drowns out its humming.

"Progress," a voice breaks in a little further on, "is dam foolish-
ness--It is a game." It is impossible to know whether the pun on "damn"
is intentional here; but the game for this man, at least, is a dangerous
one, involving even "the deeply religious friend of great men and women
in incipience" in a kind of omnivorous mania. "Hold me close, closer,
close as you can," pleads the guilty husband-lover-writer," . . . I have
been stealing. I should never touch anything. . . . I cannot stop: the
word I am seeking is in your mouth--I cannot stop. Hold me against--"
The frenzy breaks off and the writer addresses Williams' Illinois friend
and fellow-poet, Alva N. Turner, counselling him that "it may be permis-
sible to write about a poetic sweetheart but never about a wife--should
have said possible. All men do the same. Dante be damned. Knew nothing
at all. Lied to himself all his life. Profited by his luck and never
said thanks. God pulled the lady up by the roots. Never even said thank
you. Quite wrong." The style is reminiscent of Ezra Pound's in his most
irascible letters, but the real wrinkle here is the memory of Williams'
1918 essay, "Prose About Love," discussed in my first chapter. There he
specifically celebrated married love as a suitable subject for writers,
though a difficult one. Clearly there are two sides on this issue and
Williams turns his satirical attention here onto the most savage and least
loving one. The conflict rages as the writer struggles against one love
in behalf of the other and at the same time seeks a way to write the two.

"Liberate the words. You tie them. Poetic sweetheart. Ugh. Poetic sweetheart. My dear Miss Word let me hold your W. I love you." The solution
seems momentarily to be to "Dramatize myself [,] make it sing together as if
the world were a bird. . . ." But the other side breaks in with a well-
deserved "Nonsense." Finally the struggle seems on the verge of resolution, even as the mind in which it rages contemplates the end of a novel
and the clearing away of all confusion: "He had written the last word and
getting up he understood the fog as it billowed before the lights." He
goes into his wife's bedroom full of exaltation and announces that he has
"added a new chapter to the art of writing." The wife responds, "What did
you say, dear, I have been asleep." Here Williams is again employed in
poking fun both at other writers and their various creative frenzies and
at himself. The triumphant egomania of a man involved in the self-conscious act of creation cannot have been strange to him; and neither can the
sleepy responses of a wife to such impractical excitement.

Chapter Three opens with a pompous critical response to Williams'
own style in the book: "It is Joyce with a difference. The difference
being greater opacity, less erudition, reduced power of perception. . . .
No excuse for this sort of thing. Amounts to a total occlusion of intelligence. Substitution of something else. What? Well, nonsense. Since
you drive me to it." Then Williams turns the eye of his "critic" to Kora
in Hell and has him recite the familiar response of the trans-Atlantic
literateur: "Take the improvisations: what the French reader would say
is: Oui, ça; j'ai déjà vu ça; ça c'est de Rimbaud. Finis." The ironic
conclusion reached is that "representative American verse will be that

which will appear new to the French . . . prose the same."

Williams' imaginary critic challenges him to show some real "invention," asking him to let him "see what you can do with your vaunted pen."
The writer responds with a discussion of Joyce that is not altogether flat-
tering, but which concludes with a remark we can probably accept as "true"
from Williams. "But you must not mistake his real, if hidden service. He
has in some measure liberated words, freed them for their proper uses. He
has to a great measure destroyed what is known as 'literature'. For me as
an American it is his only important service."

What Williams means here by "literature" he describes later on in
the chapter as "Permanence. A great army with its tail in antiquity.
Cliché of the soul: beauty." And one of the forces he poses against this
form of literature is "art that does . . . work. . . . Revolution. Rus-
sia. Kropotkin. Farm, Factory and Field. --CRRRRRASH. --Down comes
the world." For this, the writer claims he is willing, like Orpheus or
the author of _Kora_, to risk everything, "to go down into hell," or at least
"look" there to see what can be useful.

Another force for the "revolution" is the automobile. It appears in
this chapter in the middle of all the critical discussion and makes its
own contribution after the writer-driver has maneuvered his "trusty mechanism" into his garage. "The lights continued to flare intimately against
the wooden wall as much to say:

> And what is good poetry made of
> And what is good poetry made of
> Of rats and snails and puppy-dogs tails
> And that is what good poetry is made of."

Needless to say "bad poetry" in the car's opinion, is made of "sugar and spice and everything nice." Thus the automobile becomes a kind of spokesman for the author's own attitudes, and the symbol of the America and the modernity which Williams seeks in an art divorced from the failures and the "beauty" of preceding generations. The narrator bursts out revealingly later in the book in a dialogue with a father, perhaps Williams' own father-in-law, the German-born "Pa" Herman. "Such a cuddle muddle: is that modern German poetry? I never saw such a lot of things mixed together under one title. These are modern times, Pa, airships and automobiles; you cover space--." Throughout The Great American Novel the automobile, for perhaps the first time in serious American writing, is related to aspects of escape from the past and from the ordinary, and entrance into total modernity. It is a kind of objective correlative for the new writing Williams demands of himself. It is no wonder Williams said later that the "heroine" of the book was "a little Ford car," who "falls more or less in love with a Mack truck." There is a clear meaning behind this facetiousness. The Mack truck, that "great powerful mechanism," as Williams calls it in The Great American Novel, "all in his new paint against the gutter," symbolizes America itself. The Ford car, "a hot little baby," is the "new" literature of Williams and his friends, wooing the great machine "with fluttering heart in the hope, the secret hope that perhaps, somehow he would notice--HE, the great truck in his massiveness and paint, that somehow he would come up to her."

As the car and truck continue their romance in a fog--a fog of the waste land--which is described as "a blackness, a choking smother of dirty water in suspension," the voice of the "new" continues its attack on the

literary establishment. H. G. Wells is singled out as the defender of
the status quo: "No new form of the novel required. Lack of substance
always takes the form of novelty mongering. Empire must be saved! Saved
for the proletariat." The response of the revolutionary novelist to this
paternalism is simple: "And what has anything Wells says to do with serious writing." The important task, as was the case in _Kora,_ is to purify
the language, restore it to a more natural state: "Save the words. Save
the words from themselves. They are like children. . . . They cannot,
must not, will not be mustered of the people, by the people, for the people. They will have their way."

As the argument goes on, the great red and green gasoline truck, with
the words "Standard Motor Gasoline, in capital letters" painted on its
side, continues to "discharge its gasoline into a tank buried in the ground
near the gutter." And the little car struggles up hill without attracting
the truck's attention. The American continent is busily wasting its enormous resources, Williams seems to be saying, and the "contact" between artist and raw material so essential to a culture is still not made.

In the subsequent chapter the battle between the American and the
European in contemporary art is closed. The exchanges are bitter:

> Now then, Aemilius, what is European conscious-
> ness composed of? --Tell me in one word. _Rien,_
> _rien, rien!_ It is at least very complicated.
> Oh very.
> You damned jackass. What do you know about
> Europe? Yes, what in Christ's name do you know?
> Your mouth is a sewer, a cloaca.
> Complicated consciousness quite aside from a
> possible revaluation. It has no value for ME.
> . . . .
>
> Europe is nothing to us. Simply nothing.

> Their music is death to us. We are starving--
> not dying--not dying mind you--but lean-bellied
> for words. God I would like to see some man,
> some one of the singers step out in the midst
> of some one of Aida's songs and scream like a
> puma.
> But you poor fellow, you use such inept fig-
> ures. Aida has been dead artistically in Munich
> for fifty years.

The American voice works painfully through the catalogue of complaints

against European art seeking "relief" or "release," at least some one point

when a truly American art could have a "beginning." The key seems to be

in converting a European language--and cultural heritage--into something

new. The American reasons, "We have no words. Every word we get must be

broken off from the European mass. Every word we get placed over again

by some delicate hand. Piece by piece we must loosen what we want. What

we will have. Will they let it go?" As the quest continues the tone of

the American voice becomes shriller and more personal. The statements

made become more obsessive and sweeping and less certain in their direc-

tion and conclusions. But they set Williams increasingly apart from any

"transatlantic" tradition:

> What good to talk to me of Santayana and your
> later critics. I brush them aside. They do
> not apply. . . . I am far under them. I am
> less, far less if you will. I am a beginner.
> I am an American. A United Stateser. Yes
> it's ugly, there is no word to say it better. . . .
> Ugliness is a horror to me but it is less ab-
> horrent than to be like you even in the most
> remote, the most minute particular. For the
> moment I hate you, I hate your orchestras,
> your libraries, your sciences, your yearly
> salons, your finely tuned intelligences of
> all sorts. My intelligence is as finely
> tuned as yours but it lives in hell, it is
> doomed to eternal--perhaps eternal--shift-
> ings after what? Oh to hell with Masters
> and the rest of them. To hell with every-
> thing I have myself ever written.

The final two sentences here reflect a momentary despair in even the most locally "American" writing of the time. It is difficult to evaluate Williams' response to Edgar Lee Masters, however, for to my knowledge he mentions him nowhere else in his writing.[10]

Chapter Six is devoted to examples of what it is to write out of the "cuddle muddle" of modern times and to create in doing so a portrait of America: "O America! Turn your head a little to the left please. So. Now are you ready? Watch my hand. Now: Lohengrin in ITALIAN, SUNG AT MANHATTAN--San Carlo Company Revives Wagner Opera, with Anna Fitziu as Elsa." The portrait in unmatching pigments and materials is comprised of many things. There is the sound of fire engines in the night, passing "with a crash and roar of the exhausts," while "in a thousand beds men of forty, women of thirty eight, girls in their teens, boys tired from football practice and little boys and girls down to babyhood wake and think the same thoughts. They listen and count the number of strokes, and sink back saying to themselves: Fire!"[11] Three days of rain, the sound of trees blowing in the darkness, a growing autumn chill, two men talking at a train station, men with women in momentary glimpses, a description of the swallow's bill, and a cruelly unconsummated affair between a young woman and a man "in search of a word" who instead of meeting her goes home to his wife and his "white paper"--all these make up the pastiche. And behind each of these stands the figure of the writer himself, struggling to set things down as they are, without "a word to stand on," who nevertheless continues to stand, "not knowing why."

The theme of the new and the "discovery of America" is taken up in the following chapter. In the opening lines Columbus and his sailors

land on the beaches of the "Nuevo Mundo," experiencing a "wild joy of release from torment of the mind." It is the same kind of release, of course,
that Williams mentions earlier when he is calling for a new departure in
art in his country. And he effectively illustrates its power and sense
of newness with a brief paragraph about "children released from school"
who play in autumn leaves suddenly no longer on the trees: "A new world,"
in which "more sky appeared to their eyes than ever before."

The writer ponders the growth of a new language of "words accurate
to the country," and wonders if it is "too late to be Eric." The thrust
of his concern here is obviously the same which propelled Williams to un-
dertake In the American Grain. He puts to himself the seminal question
behind his later book, chapters of which he was already at work on:

> I wonder, he said, whether it could be pos-
> sible that the influence of the climate--I
> wonder if the seed, the sperm of that, ex-
> isted in Columbus. Was it authentic? Is
> there a word to be found there? Could it be
> that in those men who had crossed, in the
> Norse as well as the Mongols, something spon-
> taneous could not have been implanted out of
> the air? Or was that declaration to be put
> to the credit of that German George? Was it
> only the result of local conditions?

He imagines "a new declaration of independence, signed by Columbus, found
in Porto Rico," which would presumably be the original document proclaiming the arrival of "the seed, the sperm" of a new culture and a new language.

The remainder of the chapter is taken up by a straightforward narrative of the border skirmishes fought by the Villistas and Mayo Indians
on one side against the Carrançistas of the Mexican regular army in November, 1916. Williams contrasts Bacomo, the leader of the Mayos, to the

English and American settlers and the Mexican army officers. His point
is that despite the savagery of the Indians, they were possessed of more
honor and humanity than their white allies. Bacomo reportedly argued with
his Villista ally Banderas over a "cocky Englishman" named Wilcox. Banderas was for "killing Wilcox and taking his wife and daughter for camp
women. But the Indian stood out against him. It seems Wilcox had at one
time given the Indians some sacks of beans when they were hard up for food.
They remembered this. It was a good thing for the three."

Williams closes Chapter Seven with a paragraph describing Columbus'
arrival on shore and first bartering and communication with the Indians
he found there. The ironic difference between the men of the Old World
with their "trunks of trifles" and those of the New, who "began to try to
communicate with these gods," is deftly pointed out. It is the vital tri-
angle among Wilcox, Banderas and Bacomo seen at its point of origin in the
"Nuevo Mundo" all will inhabit.

Having discussed the original inhabitants of America and its first
"conquerors," Williams moves on in Chapter Eight to analyze the last flowering of the Puritan mind in Mormonism. It is a complicated chapter, punc-
tuated by a short monologue apparently spoken by Williams' mother, and more
mention of the Mayo Indians. But the main thread is a chilling portrait
of Joseph Smith, Brigham Young, and their fanatical followers. The ultimate expression of the perverse and guilt-ridden Mormon experience is
the Mountain Meadow Massacre, in which a small band of gold-seekers was
murdered by Mormon settlers dressed as Indians in 1849. The Mayo Indians
are used as a contrast at the end of the chapter. Their "hostile" actions

are performed with economy and without needless violence: "A favorite trick of the Mayo Indians is, if they meet a man with good clothes, to take what they want and let him go on in his drawers."

In this chapter Williams is examining, as he does more fully in In the American Grain, the fatal differences between the "Puritan" and the "wild" inhabitants of the New World. There is never any question where his sympathies lie; yet one always senses that both components are necessary as he develops his view of "the background of America." He shows his perspective and exhibits--despite his fundamental hostility--a sympathetic understanding of the Mormon phenomenon just as clearly as he does his fascination with the Indian.

As the book procedes, Williams develops more illustrations of his "Nuevo Mundo," drawing upon history and the local scene, and giving one a distinct impression of the breadth of his reading and thinking. Many of the personalities, events or places he deals with--Aaron Burr, de Soto, Washington, the Puritan experience, the American Indian, the Cumberland plateau--are clearly related to the material in In the American Grain. Others--Greenwich Village, his grandmother, Alva Turner, Charles Demuth, the Atlantic Monthly, the local New Jersey scene, and articles from contemporary newspapers--are simply factors in Williams' own daily experience. But throughout the book one encounters the same set of preoccupations which characterize the chapters we have examined closely above. The Great American Novel must be seen as of a piece with the writing in Contact and the manifesto declared in Spring and All. It is also a sort of personal commentary on much of In the American Grain; and none

of this should be surprising when we realize that the time separation a-
mong these pieces of writing was minimal. The basic design of the book
is to drive home repeatedly by a pastiche of historical and contemporary
events and personalities the conviction that "The American background is
America. If there is to be a new world Europe must not invade us. . . .
The background of America is not Europe but America." And the assumption
about the nature of the imagination and art which allows Williams his associational mode of development in this book is close to that behind the
improvisations of Kora in Hell:

> The imagination will not down. If it is
> not a dance, a song, it becomes an outcry,
> a protest. If it is not flamboyance it be-
> comes deformity; if it is not art, it becomes
> crime. Men and women cannot be content, any
> more than children, with the mere facts of a
> humdrum life--the imagination must adorn and
> exaggerate life, must give it splendor and
> grotesqueness, beauty and infinite depth.
> And the mere acceptance of these things from
> without is not enough--it is not enough to
> agree and assert when the imagination demands
> for satisfaction creative energy. Flamboyance
> expresses faith in that energy--it is a shout
> of delight, a declaration of richness. It is
> at least the beginning of art.

Whether or not the writer is always orderly or comprehensible is never, for Williams, the ultimate test. The great aim is that America be expressed as it exists, and that the little Ford car manage its romance with
the Mack truck "to their mutual benefit." Otherwise, Williams warns us
often enough, there may soon be the very real opportunity to raise the cry
"America is lost. Ah Christ, Ah Christ that night should come so soon."

Europe is no yardstick by which the American writer should govern his
intentions or the American public should judge a man's work. If the truth

be known, as Williams finally points out, "Europe is YEARNING to see something new come out of America." As an American writer in the twentieth
century, Williams says to other writers that "it is not necessary for us
to learn from anyone but ourselves--at least it would be a relief to discover a critic who looked at American work from the American viewpoint."

The establishment of an American culture and an American art is often seen, as with the "sperm" which arrived with Columbus in Chapter Sev-
en, in sexual terms. At one point Williams proclaims that "America will
screw whom it will screw and when and how it will screw. And . . . it
will refrain from screwing when it will and . . . no amount of infiltra-
tion tactics from 'superior civilizations' can possibly make us anything
but bastards." This is Williams at his shrillest and it comes close to
self-conscious parody. But there is along with this "satire" on the A-
merican writing scene of his day a deadly serious awareness of the necessities as he sees them: "We must first isolate ourselves. Free ourselves
even more than we have. Let us learn the essentials of the American situation. . . . I know not a land except ours that has not to some small
extent made its title clear. Translate this into ancient Greek and offer
it to Harvard engraved on copper to be hung in the waterclosets which
freshmen use." Williams was to do better than that in offering America
Spring and All and In the American Grain within the next two years.

V. The Prose of _Spring and All_ (1923)

Williams looked back in 1956 on the prose portions of _Spring and All_ as "a mixture of philosophy and nonsense. It made sense to me, at least to my disturbed mind--because it was disturbed at that time--but I doubt if it made sense to anyone else."[1] It was dedicated to his friend, the Precisionist painter Charles Demuth, whom he had first known at Mrs. Chain's rooming house in Philadelphia while a medical student. Williams writes of his first encounter with Demuth in _The Great American Novel_, though he never mentions him by name. "There was something soft there, a reticence, a welcome, a loneliness that called to me. And he, he must have seen it in me too. We looked, two young men, and at once the tie was cemented. It was gaged accurately at once and sealed for all time."[2]

As James Guimond has pointed out in his excellent book, _The Art of William Carlos Williams_, there were "stylistic similarities" between the painting of Demuth and another long-time friend, Charles Sheeler, and the writing Williams was doing in the late 'teens and early twenties.[3] Guimond assigns these resemblances to "temperamental affinities," but also notes that "Demuth's art and attitude toward life--sophisticated, sharp-witted and irreverent--corresponded to Williams' taste for 'something new. . . . Something to enliven our lives by its invention, some breadth of under-standing, some lightness of touch.'"[4]

Spring and All shares with _The Great American Novel_ a difficult and provocative style and attitude.[5] It is full of the impatience which marks all Williams' prose of the period. The opening, like the opening of _The Great American Novel_, is a bald statement about the efficacy of simply setting something down without concern for formal particulars or a readership: "If anything of the moment results," writes Williams as he embarks on the book, "--so much the better. And so much the more likely will it be that no one will want to see it." Williams mentions the troublesome matter of foreign cultural traditions in slightly different terms at the outset of Spring and All, referring to them as a kind of barrier standing "between the reader and his consciousness of immediate contact with the world."

There is also here another of the familiar encounters between Williams and an anonymous critic who dresses him down for writing "antipoetry." Ironically it is the same accusation--though he meant it as a compliment-- that Wallace Stevens was to make in his Preface to Williams' Collected Poems 1921-1931, published in 1934.[6] It is easy to understand why Williams might have been "nettled" later with his friend, for his response to such a charge in Spring and All makes abundantly clear that he has "never been satisfied that the anti-poetic had any validity or [had] even existed."[7] Williams perceptively interprets the "noble apostrophe" which calls his work "the very antithesis of poetry" to be a cry of fear and anger. He feels that it really means something like: "You have robbed me. God, I am naked. What shall I do?" Discussing this reaction to new work, Williams challenges the reader to know and dare to know "what he is at the exact moment that he is. . . . This moment is the only thing in which I am at all interested." To accomplish this one must read Spring and All just as one reads Kora in Hell: as a book addressed "to the imagination." And the stated aim of Spring and All is very close to the achievement of the earlier book: "To refine, to clarify, to intensify that eternal mo- ment in which we alone live." It is an attempt by Williams to define his art clearly and concisely, and to plot his present and future aims.

Williams ends his opening remarks, however, with a plea for total union between the author and his reader. It is not a plea he has made before, and it is in quite a different tone from the one which Marianne Moore had found "disdainful" in the Prologue to Kora. We have a sense that the man who is writing in Spring and All is more secure as an artist, that he knows that he has something "of moment" to say. He actively woos the reader and makes an effort to establish real sympathetic bonds between his audience and himself: "In the imagination, we are from henceforth (so long as you read) locked in a fraternal embrace, the classic caress of author and reader. We are one. Whenever I say 'I' I mean also 'you.' And so, together, as one, we shall begin."

Because a considerable portion of the book is devoted to treating ideas we have already encountered in slightly different garb elsewhere in the writings of these years, I shall keep my discussion of the prose of Spring and All as brief as possible. I shall single out for attention only those passages which seem to me original to Spring and All or basic to our understanding of the book.

The chapters are numbered in a bizarre and confusing way to serve, Williams later said, as a "travesty on the idea" of typographical experiment.[8] There is only a rough sequential order to the chapters as they appear, and they could each be treated individually as essays without losing much coherence. Taken as a whole, however, and in conjunction with the poems scattered through the book, there is a distinct unity in Spring and All that is missing from The Great American Novel.

The earlier chapters are devoted to a development of the idea that a "new world," a "spring" has indeed arrived after an interminable process in which "through the orderly sequence of unmentionable time EVOLUTION HAS REPEATED ITSELF FROM THE BEGINNING." In one sense we may take this "evolution" as a highly personal one. It is the process by which a writer repeats and recreates himself and his previous work each time he embarks upon a new piece of work. Williams seems to be saying on one level that Spring and All is the end product of just such an "evolutionary" process, that "for the moment everything is fresh, perfect, recreated." In this book--and most specifically in the poems it contains--"the perfect effect is being witlessly discovered." The imagination, in a familiar Williams posture, "drunk with prohibitions, has destroyed and recreated everything afresh in the likeness of that which it was. Now indeed men look about in amazement at each other with a full realization of the meaning of 'art.'" That is at least what Williams hopes they will do.

He urges his reader to let go of all his usual logic, as he did in another way in the Prologue to Kora. To meet this book on its own terms one must assume the stance of the ingenue, totally opposed to those Williams refers to as "the traditionalists of plagiarism," who are like the figures in "Phidias' frieze . . . their legs advancing a millionth part of an inch every fifty thousand years." In the burgeoning of a new kind of art and a new book, "at last that process of miraculous verisimilitude, that great copying which evolution has followed, repeating move for move every move that it made in the past--is approaching the end." And with the arrival of the untitled first poem, "By the road to the contagious

hospital," later titled "Spring and All," that epoch is at an end. "THE
WORLD IS NEW." Ironically this particular poem, as Williams later noted,
"has been praised by the conventional boys for its form."[9] Thus the radical departure Williams saw himself taking in Spring and All was not, perhaps, always as strange and new as he conceived it. But this is an easi-
er evaluation to make with hindsight. Certainly the poem is an announce-
ment--whether or not its formal characteristics were acceptable to the
literary establishment. It is a statement at once about the birth of a
new order and the transformation of "objects"--their definition and clar-
ification--by the creative process. From the first line on, the effects
of a beneficial "contagion" spread through the poem, as Williams hopes
they will through all American art. "The profound change" of growth, of
springtime in a new world, has come over the landscape. The years of
searching and dismissing, of attacking and proclaiming, begin to bear
fruit.

The chapter headed "Chapter I. Samuel Butler" continues the discussion of the battle between "the traditionalists of plagiarism" and the
innovators, among whom Williams numbers himself and Demuth. Butler is
presented as a spokesman of the sort Jepson and Eliot typified in the
Prologue to Kora. His text is subtly persuasive: "There are two who can
invent some extraordinary thing to one who can properly employ that which
has been made use of before." Against this "Demuth and a few others do
their best . . . telling us that design is a function of the IMAGINATION,
describing its movements, its colors--but it is a hard battle." Williams
correctly sees himself as one of those embroiled "in the midst of the ac-

tion." In the words of his poem "The Farmer," which follows directly on this passage of prose, he is "the artist figure of/The farmer--composing/--antagonist." He jots down his "few notes . . . under distracting circumstances" to remind himself--and us--"of the truth." And he refers us back to "p. 2, paragraph 4" to reread that "truth"--the real end and meaning of the new art: "to know what [one] is at the exact moment that he is."

In a subsequent unnumbered chapter Williams further defines and elaborates on his purposes in Spring and All. In doing so he introduces the central preoccupation of the prose sections in the book, the working out of which costs him considerable effort and requires much backing and filling before he manages it. "Nothing is put down in the present book," he writes, "--except through weakness of imagination--which is not intended as of a piece with the 'nature' which Shakespeare mentions and which [Marsden] Hartley speaks of so completely in his 'Adventures': it is the common thing which is anonymously about us." And he follows this with what is for him now a basic premise concerning the writer's craft: "Composition is in no essential an escape from life."

This last statement and the passages which follow to a very real extent qualify and criticize Williams' work of the preceding years, especially the Improvisations. As he has said earlier in this same chapter, "Crude symbolism is to associate emotions with natural phenomena such as anger with lightning, flowers with love. . . . Such work is empty. It is very typical of almost all that is done by the writers who fill the pages every month. . . . Everything that I have done in the past--except those parts which may be called excellent--by chance, have that quality about

them." Williams was preparing for this new direction as he wrote in Contact and in The Great American Novel of the necessity for art to be true
to experience. In Spring and All, his aim is to create something profoundly new for himself as an artist, an art which "completes" nature in a way
which we shall examine later in this chapter. As he moves to the heart
of his current and future intentions as a writer, Williams plots out his
direction exactly. In doing so he places this book in direct opposition
to much of his earlier work.

> What I put down of value will have this
> value: an escape from crude symbolism, the
> annihilation of strained associations, com-
> plicated ritualistic forms designed to sep-
> arate the work from "reality"--such as rhyme,
> meter as meter and not as the essential of
> the work, one of its words. . . .
> The work will be in the realm of the im-
> agination as plain as the sky is to a fisher-
> man. . . . The word must be put down for it-
> self, not as a symbol of nature but a part,
> cognisant of the whole--aware--civilized.

One is reminded by the figure Williams uses for his future work here of
W. B. Yeats's earlier declaration of new intentions in such poems as "The
Fisherman," though there they had deeper political overtones. What Yeats [10]
sought in a poem "as cold/And passionate as the dawn" is not unrelated to
the simplicity and unity with experience Williams is looking for in Spring
and All. While it is unfortunately outside the scope of this essay to
discuss the poems which Williams printed in Spring and All more fully,
they are designed to exemplify those qualities.

Williams' thinking about what he is aiming for seems to become clearer as he writes in Spring and All. Presumably this is by design, although
it is interesting to note that the very act of setting down the theories

behind the poems he includes clarifies his intentions for him. The spontaneity and occasional capriciousness of the earlier chapters give way
gradually to a more firmly constructed exposition, though it may seem at
first reading to be as opaque as ever. I quote at length from a passage
which I consider central to Williams' theory of art:

> The inevitable flux of the seeing eye
> toward measuring itself by the world it in-
> habits can only result in crushing humilia-
> tion unless the individual raise himself to
> some approximate co-extension with the uni-
> verse. This is possible only by aid of the
> imagination. Only through the agency of
> this force can a man feel himself moved
> largely with sympathetic pulses at work-- 11
> A work of the imagination which fails to
> release the senses in accordance with this
> major requisite--the sympathies, the intel-
> ligence in its selective world[--] fails at
> the elucidation, the alleviation which is
> --- [true art].
> In the composition, the artist does ex-
> actly what every eye must do with life, fix
> the particular with the universality of his
> own personality--taught by the largeness of
> his imagination to feel every form which he
> sees moving within himself, he must prove
> the truth of this by expression.
> The contraction which is felt.

The theory behind the first paragraph is an ancient one: that the
artist, like all men who wish to stand free of the weight of universal
magnitude and perfection, must adopt a position which is "co-extensive"
with the Creation. This does not mean that the work of art occupies
spatial or temporal boundaries with the natural object on which it is
based, nor that during the time that he is creating the artist exists on
that natural continuum himself. Rather, as Williams points out repeatedly in Spring and All, it means that the artist "completes" nature, just
as he completes his individual life, "by the imagination." Thus the work

of art is given an existence which is not "imitative," not a "copy" of
nature, but rather a separate entity with a separate existence which accomplishes something nature cannot accomplish. The artist has stood beside nature and imitated not the natural scene, but rather the natural
process. He does not seek, nor should he, to be at one with the creative
force of the external world, but to employ correctly those "sympathetic
pulses at work" within himself through the "aid of the imagination." If
he employs these correctly he focusses external reality through the lens
of his total personality, and in doing so creates a work of art. This
focussing process is "the contraction which is felt." In his theorizing
here, Williams looks both backward to the Romantics and forward to the
notions of focus and intensity behind the "Objectivist" movement of the
1930's.

The remainder of this seminal passage is a discussion of the place
of "technique" in this process, for the question must inevitably arise
of how the artist "gets down" what he has focussed. Williams' explanation is extremely muddled, but this may be due to a seriously lacerated
text as much as to any unwillingness to close with the matter. I will
give the text as it appears in the original and then a version I have re-
constructed for the sake of greater clarity.

> All this being anterior to technique, that can have
> only a sequent value; but since all that appears to
> the senses on a work of art does so through
>   fixation by
> the imagination of the external as well internal means
> of expression the essential nature of technique or
> transcription.

What I believe we should read here is something like the following: Because the "fixing" or focussing of the particular object through the imag-

ination and personality of the artist is the first order of business, technique is only of value later on. All the data which appear to the senses in creating a work of art do so through this act of focussing or "fixing" what is present and expressible both in external reality and in the artist's mind. Therefore the essential nature of what we call technique is only the transcription of what we have so fixed into our particular medium.

Thus it is the imagination for Williams which remains in the forefront. Technique is, most plainly, what will best serve to get the fully realized work of art out upon the page, canvas, clay or instrument. This is not necessarily a wholly new idea for Williams; it is rather the setting down clearly for the first time the rules which governed his work almost from the beginning. The broken style and erratic nature of the prose written between 1917 and 1922 lend ample testimony to his habit as a writer of turning to whatever his mind brings him and using that imaginatively to fill in his narrative or amplify his point.

What this philosophy does demand of its follower, however, is a total dedication to simplicity and directness in the language chosen to express "the contraction which is felt." This is something, Williams seems to be saying in Spring and All, that he has not always been capable of in the earlier work. In language, as in the choice of material, Williams notes further on, it is essential that truly "modern" art use "the forms common to experience so as not to frighten the onlooker away but to invite him . . . : things with which he is familiar, simple things--at the same time to detach them from ordinary experience [by] the imagination."[12]

The function of the imagination is seen by Williams as one which "detaches" real or common objects--and common language--from everyday life. In art, when it has been properly done, objects "are still 'real,' they are the same things they would be [if] photographed or painted by Monet, they are recognizable as the things touched by the hands during the day, but they are seen to be in some peculiar way--detached." Williams expands on this concept of the "realism" of an art created out of the imagination "fixing" external reality and thereby "completing" nature. He turns his attention to classical art in which he feels that this imaginative process "was not necessary where the subject of art was not 'reality' but related to the 'gods'--by force or otherwise. There was no need of the 'illusion' [of reality] in such a case since there was none possible where a picture or a work represented simply the imaginative reality which existed in the mind of the onlooker. No special effort was necessary to cleave where the cleavage already existed."

The difference between classical art and modern is one which Williams had hinted at without defining--or realizing--in Improvisation XVI.2., "Giants in the dirt," discussed earlier. There are no gods any longer, merely "Hebe with a sick jaw and a cruel husband" or "Zeus . . . a country doctor without a taste for coin jingling." The deepening awareness Williams exhibits in Spring and All clarifies what has happened to art, and assigns to the artist a new task. "Today where everything is being brought into sight the realism of art has bewildered us, confused us and forced us to re-invent in order to retain that which older generations had without that effort. . . . The only realism in art is of the imagination. It is only thus that the work escapes plagiarism after nature and becomes a creation." The phrase "plagiarism after nature" further

bears out my interpretation of what Williams conceived the artist's role
to be: he is involved in a process separate from nature's yet entirely
similar to it.

In the Autobiography, Williams devotes one of his rambling anecdotal
"asides" to this same matter. He tells a story which he writes he has
"told many times," about a friend named Alanson Hartpence. A woman visiting the Daniel Gallery in New York, where Hartpence worked, was looking
at a painting. "She liked it, and seemed about to make the purchase,
walked away from it, approached it and said, finally, 'But Mr. Hartpence,
what is all that down in this left hand lower corner?' Hartpence came
up close and carefully inspected the area mentioned. Then, after further
consideration, 'That, Madam,' said he, 'is paint'."[13] To Williams the story
"marks the exact point in the transition that took place, in the world of
that time, from the appreciation of a work of art as a copying of nature
to the thought of it as the imitation of nature, spoken of by Aristotle
in his Poetics, which has since governed our conceptions."[14] It was in
Spring and All that Williams first realized that this major "transition"
was occurring. In the Autobiography he treats it more fully, and with the
experience of the intervening years to add weight to his argument:

> Braque is said to have taken his pictures out-
> doors, on occasion, to see if their invention
> ranked beside that of nature worthily enough
> for him to approve of it.
> Almost no one seems to realize that this
> movement is straight from the Poetics, misin-
> terpreted for over two thousand years and more.
> The objective is not to copy nature and nev-
> er was, but to imitate nature, which involved
> active invention. . . . A man makes a picture,
> it is made of paint upon canvas stretched on
> a frame. In spite of endless talk, this has
> never been sufficiently brought out. . . . We

> have, above all, for our own Occidental thought,
> Shakespeare's "To hold a mirror up to nature"--
> as vicious a piece of bad advice as the budding
> artist ever gazed upon. . . . It is NOT to hold
> a mirror up to nature that the artist performs
> his work. It is to make, out of the imagination,
> something not at all a copy of nature, but some-
> thing quite different, a new thing, unlike any
> thing else in nature, a thing advanced and apart
> from it. 15

The fact that this entry comes in the _Autobiography_ in the chapter "Home
Again" may give us a clue as to where Williams picked up his Aristotelian
argument, which does not appear at all in _Spring_ _and_ _All_, though the re-
buke of "Shakespeare's familiar aphorism" does. On the European trip of
1924 so thoroughly chronicled in the chapters preceding this in the _Auto-
biography_, Williams met James Joyce several times, and they had ample opportunity to talk. It seems reasonable to assume that Joyce saw _Spring
and All_,which had been published in Paris by McAlmon and Bird several
months before Williams' arrival, or had at least been told about it in
some detail by one or another of those who took an interest in both men--
possibly McAlmon.

In the "Paris Notebook" entry for 27 March, 1903, a youthful Joyce
takes up the translation of "_e_ _tekhne_ _mimeitai_ _ten_ _physin_" from Aristotle.
"This phrase is falsely rendered as 'Art is an imitation of Nature'.
Aristotle does not here define art; he says only, 'Art imitates Nature'
and means that the artistic process is like the natural process. . . ." [16]
It is quite conceivable that Joyce gave Williams the argument from Aristotle to chew over during the latter's Paris visit, for certainly it did
not occur to Williams to argue from classical texts in his early formula-
tion of the difference between copying and imitation.

Further on in the same section of Spring and All, Williams undertakes
an appraisal of his own previous work in light of what he now feels to be
true about art. As is usually the case when an artist looks back, he finds
it not altogether satisfactory. But he is sensible enough to realize that
what he was doing in the earlier books--most especially in Kora--was all
part of a learning process. At best it never fell into Anatole France's
category of art as "lies." He recognizes that he has often been unclear
in his writing, moving "chaotically about refusing or rejecting most things,
seldom accepting values or acknowledging anything . . . because I early
recognized the futility of acquisitive understanding and at the same time
rejected religious dogmatism." He confesses that "being of a slow but
accurate understanding," he has "not always been able to complete the intellectual steps" which would have made him firm in the conviction of the
worth and power of "works of the imagination."

He explains that in Kora in Hell he "let the imagination have its
own way to see if it could save itself," and that he "began then and there
to revalue experience, to understand where I was at--." He praises the
improvisations' "placement in a world of new values," but finds fault with
"their dislocation of sense, often complete." He is, if anything, too
hard on Kora, for it succeeds better than he realized in giving one a
sense of a "real" but "separate" existence of things, as I have tried to
show. There is much in the earlier work, in fact, which answers perfectly the accusation that art is a lie with just the formula Williams demanded: material which "may be represented actually," but which has a
"separate existence." The difficulty with Kora is that Williams was there
struggling to express material that is too heavily "internal" and too lit-

tle "external." This is what provides the casual reader of that book with his "dislocation of sense," often too great a one to permit the mind to penetrate the opacity which results.

The aim as Williams now sees it is very close to what he was seeking in the "spontaneity" of the improvisations, but it is better planned and has more complex implications. One holds back as one writes, never attempting "to set values on the word being used, according to presupposed measures, but to write down that which happens at that time--." Thus the writer keeps himself in a state of "imaginative suspense." The difference Williams sees between the earlier work and his new program is that "Writing is not a searching about in the daily experience for apt similes and pretty thoughts. . . . It is not a conscious recording of the day's experience 'freshly and with the appearance of reality.'" Rather in writing one should "perfect the ability to record at the moment when the consciousness is enlarged by the sympathies and the unity of understanding which the imagination gives." To follow the earlier mode of writing "is seriously [detrimental] to the development of any ability in a man, it fastens him down . . . makes nature an accessory to the particular theory he is following."

Thus Williams has moved very perceptibly from the earlier theoretical stance in which he rooted his work in experience. One recalls the autobiographical sketch "The Doctor" of 1918, in which he wrote that he made his rounds "practicing my illicit trade of smelling, seeing, hearing, touching, tasting, weighing," using his professional life as a basis for his craft as a writer. This is the framework in which Kora was written. The writer of Spring and All, the writer "of imagination" would optimally be "released from observing things for the purpose of writing them down later." He would also be freed of the guilt of "stealing in order to write words" mentioned in The Great American Novel. He would depend solely on nature and his own imaginative response to it, and this would render him effectively "independent--moving at will from one thing to another--as he pleases, unbound--complete."

Though he forgets it later, in the Autobiography, Williams does not overlook the fact in Spring and All that "it is not [Shakespeare] speaking but an imaginative character of his" who advises us to hold a mirror up to nature.[17] He argues that Shakespeare, despite this bad piece of advice, "is the most conspicuous example desirable of the falseness of this very thing. He holds no mirror up to nature but with his imagination rivals nature's composition with his own." This, of course, is precisely what Williams seeks from modern artists.

Interestingly enough, his description of Shakespeare in Spring and All bears an extraordinary resemblance to Williams' own life during this period: " . . . he was a comparatively uninformed man, quite according to the orthodox tradition, who lived from first to last a life of amusing regularity and simplicity, a house and wife in the suburbs, delightful children, a girl at court (whom he really never confused with his writing) and a cafe life which gave him with the freshness of discovery, the information upon which his imagination fed. London was full of the concentrates of science and adventure." If we substitute New York for London here we have the rudimentary outlines of Williams' life in Rutherford.[18]

In discussing Shakespeare, Williams' makes the observation that "it is rarely understood how such plays" as his were written, "or in fact how any work of value has been written." His answer to this problem is the premise which underlies In the American Grain: "only as the work was produced, in that way alone can it be understood." The writing of a play is as much an historical act as the discovery of America or the founding of Kentucky, and Williams in effect outlines here the program which he was to follow in writing his most ambitious prose work over the next two years: "First must come the transposition of the faculties to the only world of reality that men know: the world of the imagination, wholly our own. From this world alone does the work gain power, its soil the only one whose chemistry is perfect to the purpose."

As this avenue of thought stretches out, the real nature of the difference between prose and poetry, and the results that should be demanded or expected of each one, become matters for careful attention. "Prose," writes Williams, "has to do with the fact of an emotion; poetry has to do with the dynamisation of emotion into a separate form." This "dynamisation" is accomplished by the "force of imagination." This is a discovery--or a formulization--of the greatest importance. It accomplishes two things for Williams: it makes the "prose-poetry" of Kora distinctly a thing of the past for him formally; and it points the direction for the future. The passage is an exciting one because in its rapid development and jerky movement it gives us an accurate reflection of Williams' mind gnawing at a problem, solving it and embellishing upon that solution:

> prose: statement of facts concerning emotions, intellectual states, data of all sorts--technical expositions, jargon, of all sorts--fictional and other--
>
> poetry: new form dealt with as a reality in itself.

The form of prose is the accuracy of its
subject matter--how best to expose the
multiform phases of its material.

the form of poetry is related to the
movements of the imagination revealed in
words--or whatever it may be--

the cleavage is complete

Why should I go further than I am able?
Is it not enough for you that I am perfect?

The cleavage goes through all the phases
of experience. It is the jump from prose to
the process of imagination that is the next
great leap of the intelligence--from the
simulations of present experience to the
facts of the imagination--
. . . .

I mean that there will always be prose
painting, representative work, clever as
may be in revealing new phases of emotional research presented on the surface.

But the jump from that to Cezanne or
back to certain of the primitives is the
impossible.

The statements regarding the "forms" of poetry and prose above are

somewhat vague; and because an understanding of these is essential to our

understanding of Williams' development as a prose writer from this time

on, I shall try to clarify them as fully as possible. Poetry, Williams

says here, is dependent for its form solely upon rules of the imagination:

the rules which the poem creates for itself as it is invented. Its form

has only to "complete" the process of the creation of a new entity, a new

object. Prose, on the other hand, is formally governed by the nature of

its subject-matter and the consideration of how best that may be commu-

nicated. It is shaped, therefore, by considerations wholly outside the completely imaginary world of the poem, even if its subject-matter is new or experimental. Prose deals with a pre-determined world, a world which exists or which has existed. Poetry deals with a world which is wholly undetermined, wholly independent from external reality and having its origin solely in "the facts of the imagination." Poetry must therefore be allowed to create its own form, without consideration of its conformity to our expectations. In painting, the work of Cezanne represented a movement toward the sort of wholly "independent" art Williams is talking about in poetry, just as many of the older primitives produced work that existed in and of itself, wholly in the world of the imagination without being of necessity "illusion," that is without trying to be "true to life." Williams' model for the painting of the future is the work of Juan Gris. This represents the real breakthrough into an area where "illusion" can be "dispensed with" and "painting has this problem before it. To replace not the forms but the reality of experience with its own [reality]."

Several pages further on Williams returns to the differentiation between prose and poetry and concentrates on what prose can do and how it should be used. "There is no need for it to approach poetry except to be weakened . . . ," writes Williams. "I expect to see prose be prose . . . relieved of its extraneous unrelated values." Its sole purpose is "clarity to enlighten the understanding. . . . If prose is not accurately adjusted to the exposition of facts it does not exist -- Its form is that alone. To penetrate everywhere with enlightenment --" In some ways this definition of what prose should be concerned with is even clearer than Williams' program for poetry, which "has to do with

the crystallization of the imagination--the perfection of new forms as
additions to nature--." Prose is essentially reportage, the presentation
of data gathered and digested to enlighten the reader.

Williams continues to worry the matter, fastening his attention on
his own writing in Spring and All:

> Is what I have written prose? The only
> answer is that form in prose ends with the
> end of that which is being communicated --
> If the power to go on falters in the middle
> of a sentence -- that is the end of the sen-
> tence -- Or if a new phase enters at that
> point it is only stupidity to go on.
>
> There is no confusion -- only difficulties.

Certainly there are numerous "difficulties" arising from his broken style
in Spring and All; but Williams manages to arrive at some very important
conclusions by gripping the problems tenaciously and working them over
as he goes. The effect is accretive, for as he realizes, prose can be
used as an "acquisitive--PROGRESSIVE force." His discussion of the met-
rical considerations of prose and poetry is particularly fine, and extremely important to anyone interested in modern writing. He argues that "it
is ridiculous to say that verse grades off into prose as the rhythm becomes less and less pronounced, in fact, that verse differs from prose
in that the meter is more pronounced, that the movement is more impas-
sioned and that rhythmical prose, so called, occupies a middle ground
between prose and verse." As he has already pointed out, prose and verse
are of a different nature entirely and "meter has nothing to do with the
question whatever." The argument from meter is for Williams very like
saying that as an apple shades toward the yellow end of the spectrum it
becomes an orange: "When poetry fails it does not become prose but bad

poetry."

In reading or "discovering" literature, Williams searches for "something" which moves him in a certain way. This "something" is difficult for him to define, and he is awkward in moving toward it. He singles out Marianne Moore as the one among "all American writers most constantly a poet . . . because the purpose of her work is invariably from the source from which poetry starts -- that it is constantly from the purpose of poetry." That purpose, despite the fact that her lines are often "diagramatically informative" rather than "full of imagery," is to "feed the imagination," to "liberate the words from their emotional implications." The true test of a good poem, he states further on, is that its words "move independently when set free." For Williams this is the basis of the new--and the correct--in poetry. In arriving at this viewpoint, he incidentally has defined for himself what is new and correct in prose.

In Spring and All, Williams' task is "to free the world of fact from the impositions of 'art' . . . . And to liberate the man to act in whatever direction his disposition leads." As he makes this summary statement he refers us to "Hartley's last chapter" in Adventures in the Arts, which is entitled "The Importance of Being 'Dada.'" In that essay, Hartley says that one effect of Dada-ism is

> to deliver art from the clutches of its worshippers, and by worshippers I mean the idolaters and the commercialists of art. By the idolaters I mean those whose reverence for art is beyond their knowledge of it. By the commercialists I mean those who prey upon the ignorance of the unsophisticated, with pictures created by the esthetic habit of, or better to say, through the banality of, "artistic" temperament. Art is at present a

> species of vice in America, and it sorely and
> conspicuously needs prohibition or interfer-
> ence. . . .
> . . . .
> We must all learn what art really is. . . .[19]

Spring and All was in part Williams' response to the challenge issued
by Hartley. In writing it he clarified for himself what he was trying to
do as a poet, and the poems in this book stand as examples of his stated
aims. In establishing those aims he managed to free prose from poetry
and set for himself a goal as a writer of prose and as a poet.

VI. <u>In the American Grain</u> (1925)

Through good fortune, good planning, or a little of both, the end
of the <u>Contact</u> period coincided precisely with the start of a "sabbati-
cal" year Williams and his wife had long planned.[1] They made arrangements
for the care of their two boys and sent them off to camp for the summer.
Williams handed on his patients to other physicians in the area, including a cousin of his and his wife--both doctors--who were to occupy the
house at 9 Ridge Road. Then the Williamses moved into the apartment of
a friend in New York and the reading and research for <u>In the American
Grain</u> got underway in earnest. The idea for the book had occurred to
Williams at least as early as 1922, as I have mentioned, and he had already published three chapters in Alfred Kreymborg's and Harold Loeb's
<u>Broom</u>, printed abroad, in early 1923.[2] His conception was that the book
should serve as "a study to try to find out for myself what the land of
my more or less accidental birth might signify. . . . The plan was to
try to get inside the heads of some of the American founders or 'heroes,'
if you will, by examining their original records."[3] The writing of the
book was to occupy much of his time over a period of two years and while
he said long afterwards that "the whole book was written in an excited
frame of mind,"[4] there is evidence that he sometimes found the project more
a task than a pleasure. Evidently thinking back on it in 1926, he wrote
to Ezra Pound, "Hell,--somedays I can write what I want to and some days
I write <u>In the American Grain</u>--and when I'm very low I can write a letter."[5] He worked regularly at the New York Public Library, reading whatever he could find that seemed appropriate and informative as source ma-

terial for each section. His aim was to get as close to the essential
spirit of the historical figures or events as possible: "I wanted nothing to get between me and what they themselves had recorded: a translation of a Norse saga, The Long Island Book, the case of Eric the Red,
would be the beginning; Columbus' Journal; the letters of Hernando Cortez to Philip of Spain; Daniel Boone's autobiography; and so forth, to a
letter, entire, written by John Paul Jones on board the Bonhomme Richard,
after his battle with the Serapis."[6]

The result could have been a kind of historical bouillabaisse, but
the book has a remarkable unity despite the variety of styles in its pages.
The chief agent of that unity is Williams' own prose. In In the American
Grain he began to put his theories expressed in Spring and All to work,
using prose to deal with facts and events--a prose governed throughout the
book by the nature of its subject matter. The result, with only occasional lapses, is a far greater degree of objectification and clarity of focus
than had been the case in the writings of the Contact years. It is very
much a new kind of writing for Williams: impressionistic, but firmly an-
chored in historical events rather than in the twilit realities of the
mind of the creator. What Williams had discovered in Spring and All was
that prose and poetry are respectively appropriate to different areas of
experience and expression. With In the American Grain he sought to root
his prose more completely in the real world and to move away from the
imaginative associational style of the previous years. At his best, he
achieves this.

The book was published by the Boni brothers in 1925 but did not en-
joy much public success. It did however attract the attention and earn

the esteem of some of the most creative people in America at the time,
among them D. H. Lawrence, Kenneth Burke, Hart Crane, Alfred Stieglitz,
Charles Sheeler, and Martha Graham.[7] Since its republication by New Directions in 1939 with an Introduction by Horace Gregory, it has gone
through many editions and its reputation has grown steadily. In his en-
cyclopedic study of the decade between the First War and the Crash, The
Twenties, Frederick J. Hoffman calls it, "Perhaps the most illuminating,
and one of the most influential, of native impressionistic readings of
American history."[8]

   Above all, In the American Grain is an attempt, as James Guimond
points out, to present to Americans a "'usable past' . . . to discover
how their modes of behavior were reborn in the past and may yet be reborn
again in the present."[9] But it is also a colloquium of voices and attitudes which have specific relevance to the personal and artistic stance
Williams was working out for himself at the time. The discovery and
development of America are analogous to the artist's own discovery of appropriate material for art and the development of his technique. To the
mind at work behind In the American Grain, it is clear that those who are
most successful as Americans are those like Williams himself, who manage
to stay in touch with their environment, to know their "place" for what
it is, to love it and express it in their lives and work.

   Beyond this, In the American Grain makes clear that the great historical, like the great artistic figure must be willing to go through
the taxing process of continuous renewal and development, undertaking
the responsibilities of his freedom and always pushing forward to break
the strictures of the prevailing modes of political or artistic expres-

sion. Among those in the book who remain true to these necessities and achieve a measure of triumph are Père Sebastian Rasles, Aaron Burr, Daniel Boone and Sam Houston; and in another mode, Red Eric and the native Americans, Montezuma and Jacataqua. Because they have made the choice for a self allied with a natural methodology they are all at one time or another outlaws or renegades, enemies of whatever establishment or notion of progress their times provide.

These people and others whom Guimond calls "the idealists"--Columbus, DeSoto, Raleigh, Champlain and Poe--are all types of the creator to one degree or another. Their success as innovators or discoverers hinges on the extent to which they can achieve the desirable balance between ideas and the natural order. The latter group--Guimond's "idealists"--all have about their lives the kind of tragedy that attends those whose achievements fall too far short of their designs.

Ranged against the figures who try to know America in her truest and most essential form are some who seem to Williams to be bent on destroying the natural order and the land or people which are its manifestations. These include most of the Conquistadors, the Puritans and those men responsible in large part for the institutionalization--and for Williams the betrayal--of the American Revolution: Franklin and Hamilton. Others, like Longfellow, Lowell and Bryant, who lurk in the background of the Poe chapter, are literary types of that same intelligence. The "enemy" then, to Williams, are plunderers, hypocrites and reactionaries whose drives and interests demand that they resist the new or the unknown and continue to subjugate the natural, political or artistic order for their own advantage.

The original dust jacket of the Boni edition carried a statement by

the author about his purpose. In subsequent editions the statement has
been printed as a prefatory note. In it Williams stresses his search for
the "true character" of his subjects. His principle attempt he writes is
"to re-name the things seen, now lost in chaos of borrowed titles, many
of them inappropriate. . . . Everywhere I have tried to separate out from
the original records some flavor of an actual peculiarity the character
denoting shape which the unique force has given." That is somewhat opaque,
especially for a jacket blurb, and it is not surprising that the sale of
the book was small. It seems ironic in retrospect that Williams and the
Bonis should have permitted the book to go into the world not simply un-
aided but with an added burden. The meaning behind this syntactical jumble, however, is essential to understanding In the American Grain. The
aim is almost a Dickensian one--to identify the true nature of an event
or a personality by illuminating that aspect which is peculiar and unique
to it.

Thus it is Eric's barbarism and primitivism that Williams stresses
in the first chapter stylistically and structurally.[10] These qualities of
the Norse explorers were not new to Williams. They had fascinated him for
years in the two descendants of the Northmen best known to him, his mother-
in-law and his wife, as the Stecher trilogy subsequently makes clear.[11] The
basic thrust of Eric's personality is spelled out clearly at the outset:
"Rather the ice than their way: to take what is mine by single strength,
theirs by the crookedness of their law." This thrust, this stubborn self-
interest and total self-reliance is a thread running through the lives of
several figures in the book. Daniel Boone, Aaron Burr and Sam Houston
all achieve their goals or live through adversity by "single strength."

And it is important to add here that Williams' choice of heroes who aim to fulfill their ambitions by going it alone tells us much about his own state of mind and helps explain the shape of his career as a writer.

The style that Williams uses in filling out Eric's personality from the records of The Long Island Book is particularly well-suited to expressing the character he perceived. The prose consists of terse, disjointed narrative virtually without descriptive passages. The closeness of the man to his environment and to his own humanity are brought out in the second paragraph. Eric notes simply that he is not "evil, but more in accord with our own blood" than those who have hounded him out of his ancestral home and then out of Iceland. "This very part of me, by their trickery must not appear, unless in their jacket," he continues. "Eric was Greenland. . . ." Eric's life, like his prose, is straightforward and primitive. It moves in whatever direction is required with intensity and total commitment: "Eric loves his friends, loves bed, loves food, loves the hunt, loves his sons. He is a man that can throw a spear, take a girl, steer a ship, till the soil, plant, care for the cattle, skin a fox, sing, dance, run, wrestle, climb, swim like a seal." He is, however, not without remarkable moments of acute perception about himself: "Hardship lives in me. What I suffer is myself that outraces the water or the wind."

Like a Ulysses unable after all to make the final journey, or like Moses on Sinai, Eric has to watch others younger than himself move on to the land of promise and challenge. Chief among these to Eric's mind is his daughter, Freydis--a personality that presumably gratified Williams' feelings about Scandanavian women. In the first fight with the natives of the New World, called "Skrellings" by the Vikings, Freydis proves her mettle and her blood. "Lagging behind the rest as they ran, because of her belly, she being with child, she found a dead man in front of her. It was Snorri's son, with his head cleft by a stone, his naked sword beside him. This she took up and prepared to defend herself. The Skrellings then approached her, whereupon she stripped down her shirt and slapped her breast with her bare sword. At this the Skrellings were terrified and ran down to their boats." "Eric in Freydis' bones," observes her father. She has strength, persuasiveness, a good mind for planning and above all is interested in herself and her own power: a suitable daughter for the great Viking renegade. But Eric's last words predict for his survivors the same hardship and evil reputation that have been his lot. The chapter ends with his final blunt statement, "Eric in his grave."

In delineating the primitive Scandinavian character the unique qualities Williams brings forth are ruthlessness, savagery and self-service. They are qualities largely lacking in Christopher Columbus, the subject of the second chapter in the book, "The Discovery of the Indies." The results are, for Columbus, disastrous. Williams has two stories to tell in this chapter, and their balance and arrangement caused him a great deal of concern. As he notes in the opening paragraph, "It is as the achievement of a flower, pure, white, waxlike and fragrant, that Columbus' infatuated course must be depicted, especially when compared with the acrid and poisonous apple which was later by him to be proved." Both stories, that of the discovery of the flower and the subsequent degradation and pain of the apple, are of importance. But the discovery is the one great and unique occurrence of Columbus' life and it was that which Williams had to stress in the chapter for a variety of reasons.

Columbus' discovery of the Indies, as I have said earlier, corresponds to the writer's discovery of his material and his theme, in short to his initial great moment of inspiration. And Columbus' total experience as presented in In the American Grain corresponds in an interesting fashion to Williams' own as a writer. As personalities their humility and delight in the face of the new and the beautiful are the same; and their passionate concern with the idea of America--for Williams the idea of American writing--meets the same inimical rebuffs from those in power or from those whose ambition is greater than their idealism. The Columbus who is humiliated and wedged out of his "new Heaven and Earth" is not unrelated to the young poet who watched others, notably Eliot, walk away with the honors after spending years trying to set American poetry on a new course. Nor are Columbus' pleas to court unlike those of Williams to friends and supporters as he watched one little magazine after another sacrificed to apathy. The chief difference, perhaps, is that Williams dared to be angrier than did Columbus. For both men one matter of grave importance is the renewal, the rediscovery, the turning one's face toward America yet another time, in search again of the great discovery.[12]

The real effectiveness of the Columbus chapter hinges, as its writer realized, on the fact that the great discovery itself is kept for the end. Williams was proud of his achievement, for to him this odd reversal of chronology in "The Discovery of the Indies" said a great deal about a whole philosophy of life and art. As he said in I Wanted to Write a Poem, "I used the Columbus Journal, and I had a devil of a job making the chapter end with the discovery. Waldo Frank was the only person who recognized the technical difficulty and [he] wrote me a letter praising the

ending. I had managed after all kinds of rewriting to tell about the three
voyages and at the same time to keep the discovery that occurred in the
first voyage for a dramatic ending. It meant turning everything around,
ending with the beginning."[13] The notion of ending with the beginning was
not new to Williams, it seems in fact to have been a dominant one throughout his life. We have encountered it in his choice of the cyclical myth
of Kora to frame his improvisations, and also in the text of Spring and
All.

What crippled Columbus, as Williams saw him, was his inability to
be a part of the New World he had discovered. Rather than integrating
himself into it, "he strove to fasten to himself that enormous world, that
presently crushed him among its multiple small disguises." Columbus' de-
ficiency was his inability to adjust his vision and his way of life to fit
a profoundly new experience. "With its archaic smile," notes the narrator,
"America found Columbus its first victim. This was well, even merciful."
Columbus chose to dwell among idealities, among dreams of becoming Don
Cristoforo, "Chief Admiral of the Ocean Sea, perpetual Viceroy and Gover-
nor of all the islands and continents that I should discover and gain in
the Ocean Sea, and that my eldest son should succeed, and so from generation to generation forever." This is his downfall, for his dream blinds
him to the practicalities of court politics and ruthlessness of his fellow explorers and pretenders to power in the new lands. This blindness,
this cutting of self off from the reality around one was very much a concern to Williams all his life. His own impatience, disgust and even anger
with the patients of "Guinea Hill" threatened continually to cut him off
from the real. The tension between the real and ideal, between the butch-

er and the Greek hero, the park's occupants and the library's stagnation never ceased to mould Williams' life and art.

Having landed at last at the Indies, the great discovery made, Columbus waits for his men to return with fresh water. "During that time I walked among the trees which was the most beautiful thing which I had ever seen. . . ." What propelled Williams was his ultimate willingness to accept and love the "beautiful thing" which to Columbus as much as to Paterson himself was and is the raw essence of America.

Like De Flores' pursuit of Beatrice in The Changeling, Europe ravened after Columbus' discovery. Williams' perception of the reasons produces one of the most startling and memorable passages of In the American Grain: "Upon the orchidean beauty of the new world the old rushed inevitably to revenge itself after the Italian's return. Such things occur in secret. Though men may be possessed by beauty while they work that is all they know of it or of their own terrible hands; they do not fathom the forces which carry them." This is the opening of Williams' third chapter, "The Destruction of Tenochtitlan." Cortez' men, "the pack whom the dead drive," as Williams calls them, confront and destroy what was at the time probably the most beautiful city in the world. At their backs is "The evil of the whole world . . . the perennial disappointment which follows, like smoke, the bursting of ideas . . . the spirit of malice which underlies men's lives and against which nothing offers resistance." To Williams Cortez was "neither malicious, stupid nor blind, but a conqueror like other conquerors," and it was his "appetite for the adventure" that forced the Spanish on the Aztecs. The ultimate conflict between the two cultures occurred over gold, though the underlying differences between them are

most clearly revealed in the Spaniards' reaction to Aztec religious prac-
tices. The human sacrifices in pitch-black chapels were only a symptom
of the Indians' radically different orientation. Williams' insights into native Central American life-styles which conflicted so dynamically
with those of the known world have seldom been matched by a creative artist, though Charles Olson deals with the same subject-matter very effectively in his poem "The Kingfishers" and in his Mayan Letters.[14] Williams
points out "the earthward thrust" of the Indians' logic, "blood and earth;
the realization of their primal and continuous identity with the ground
itself, where everything is fixed in darkness. The priests in black robes,
tribal men, never cutting or combing the hair; the instinctive exclusion
of women from all places of worship; the debarring of priests from female
society: it was a ceremonial acknowledgment of the deep sexless urge of
life itself, the hungry animal, underlying all other power. . . ."

Throughout the chapter Williams stresses Cortez' reluctance to "force"
the Indians' hand, his horror and dejection over the recalcitrance which
causes their massacre and the destruction of their city. The attempts
of Montezuma to save his city—Williams knew nothing apparently of the
myth of Quetzalcoatl—are treated as extraordinary and mysterious, but the
reasons offered are perceptive and humane.[15] "Perhaps by a sudden daring
stroke this man might have rid himself of the intestine enemy. . . . Perhaps fear had unmanned him. Perhaps what we call forbearance was no more
than the timidity which is an overwhelming agony of heart inspired by the
sight of a resistless force aimed at our destruction. Still, if this be
so, Montezuma has left no trace of cowardice upon the records." Montezuma's
death and the ultimate destruction of the city are, whatever the circum-

stances, seen by Williams as the inevitable result of confrontation between two totally alien cultures.

Williams' chapter on Ponce de Leon, "The Fountain of Eternal Youth,"
is not one of his best, probably because Ponce's life lacked the spirit
of grand adventure present in the lives of the greater discoverers and
Conquistadores. Ponce's story—or what there is of it here—is told in
a style that is, in Williams' words, "lyrical, extravagant, romantic on
purpose."[16] But the chapter begins with a tone foreign to the first section of the book—an outburst reminiscent of The Great American Novel.
Horace Gregory found the opening sentences of sufficient provocative value
to include them in his Introduction. "History, history!" ejaculates Williams in an angry voice. "We fools, what do we know or care? History
begins for us with murder and enslavement, not with discovery. No, we
are not Indians but we are men of their world. The blood means nothing;
the spirit, the ghost of the land moves in the blood, moves the blood.
It is we who ran to the shore naked, we who cried, 'Heavenly Man!'" Despite the flamboyance of its rhetoric, the passage contains at least one
idea which is of importance to any reading of In the American Grain: we
share with the Indians this continent; their world as it was also conditions us now and makes all Americans unique among members of other cultures.
This is a romantic notion, admittedly, but it is the one that gives Williams
his "snapper" in the chapter. For having made this assertion he goes on
to show, with Ponce's cruel, self-interested life, that we are in fact a
culture horribly divided against ourselves and that there has been from
the first brutality and treachery on the part of both aboriginals and in-
vaders. We who are the descendants of this first conflict still suffer

spiritual division, for we remain enthralled by the dark spirit of the primitive Americans: "Fierce and implacable we kill them," writes Williams, "but their souls dominate us. Our men, our blood, but their spirit is master. It enters us, it defeats us, it imposes itself. We are moderns--madmen at Paris--all lacking in a ground sense of cleanliness."

Williams juggles chronology in this chapter as well, but without the dramatic success he achieves in the Columbus chapter. He recites the story of the massacre of the laundresses and the death of Ponce's dog, Berrescien, which took place on the penultimate voyage of the search itself, early in the chapter. Then he returns at the end to Ponce's final journeys and his death. The only reason for the shape of the narrative sequence is to suit Williams' rhetorical needs; the structure does not seem to grow organically from the real nature of Ponce or his experience, as had been the case with Columbus. The chapter is formally less true to the events, the facts, the essence of what Williams is trying to get at, and as a result it is the least successful among the earlier group.

In his treatment of "de Soto and the New World," however, Williams remains entirely true to his historical conception of de Soto. The "She" who woos the explorer on to his death beside the greatest of all American rivers is a sort of feminized version of D. H. Lawrence's "aboriginal demon hovering over the core of the continent."[17] Williams' metaphor for the destructive power of the great wilderness is that of the insatiable seductress--a kind of massive but invisible Circe tempting men to spend themselves in her exhausting embrace.

Even as de Soto crosses the Mississippi for the first time, taking the New World by his superior force and technology, the spirit that Wil-

liams has created warns him of her power: "But you are mine and I will
strip you naked--jealous of everything that touches you. Down, down to
me--in and under and down, unbeaten, the white kernel, the flame--the flame
burning under water, that I cannot quench."

The "orchidean beauty" of the New World, then, has something about
it, like the flower itself, that is darkly and powerfully sexual. And
this is a kind of sexuality which is fundamentally inviolable in Williams'
view. It takes what it needs from men, giving them only exhaustion and
despondency in return. Even in the metaphorical consummation there exists
no unity between the explorer and his greatest conquest. "She" remains
"formless" and "liquid," elementally separate from the unquenchable flame
of de Soto's ambition and drive--the power which stands behind his great
thrust toward the heart of the continent. Committed to the waters of the
river, de Soto's shrouded body sinks "down, this solitary sperm, down into
the liquid, the formless, the insatiable belly of sleep." Echoing the
uncaring river itself and the spirit behind it, Williams' prose suddenly
reverts to a description of the fishes of the Mississippi, reporting apparently verbatim from his source material. De Soto's death ends the dialogue of a strong man with the dark spirit of the Americas. What is left,
like the wind or rush of the water, is only the unemotional sequence of
natural and historical description:

> There was likewise a kind called peel-fish,
> the snout a cubit in length, the upper lip
> being shaped like a shovel. Others were like
> a shad. There was one called pereo the Indi-
> ans brought, the size of a hog and had rows
> of teeth above and below.
> Luis de Moscosco ordered the property of
> the Governor to be sold at public cry. It

> consisted of two male and three female
> slaves, three horses, and seven hundred
> swine. From that time forward most of
> the people owned and raised hogs.

Sir Walter Raleigh, in Williams' chapter on him, is also a man used up by the implacable female principle; but this time the principle is embodied in the figure of Elizabeth I. In Williams' hands Raleigh becomes a man "made and cracked by majesty." His mission to the Americas becomes "a voyage on the body of his Queen: England, Elizabeth--Virginia!" New World and Old become allies in his destruction, for his major flaw, like Columbus', is that his vision of the American reality is too gravely tempered by the European ones in which he has lived.

The prose of the chapter is, as Selden Rodman perceived and Williams himself observed in a letter to him, "exceptionally regular in its meter," so regular in fact that Rodman included it in his One Hundred Modern Poems.[18] Williams went on to say that he'd never looked at it "as anything but what it set out to be: an 'imitation' of Raleigh, Raleigh caught in the mesh of his own period's forms." But in style the piece can hardly be said to be Elizabethan in the best sense. It is filled with stiff and inflated rhetoric and broken repeatedly by apostrophes to the Muse. It is never quite clear from the figure of Raleigh that emerges whether Clio, Melpomene or Euterpe is the Muse addressed. Presumably Williams intends us to opt for tragedy here, but there are too many unanswered questions about Raleigh to be sure: "Why did he send his son into that tropic jungle and not go himself. . . . And when the boy had died why not die too? Why England again and force the new king to keep his promise and behead him?" The reader is left with the feeling that while Williams' heart may have

been in this chapter, his intellectual grasp of the man as he really was
wavered as he dealt with him. Raleigh hardly seems to have been as mysterious a figure as Williams would have the Muse believe: "that lost man:
seer who failed, planter who never planted, poet whose works are questioned,
leader without command, favorite deposed—but one who yet gave title for
his Queen, his England, to a coast he never saw but grazed alone with
genius."

In his attitude toward the Puritans, Williams shared the largely in-
accurate views of those in the 1920's who condemned them roundly, following Randolph Bourne and H. L. Mencken among others.[19] In the "Voyage of the
Mayflower," he sees them as the "seed of Tudor England's lusty blossoming. The flamboyant force of that zenith, spent, became in them hard and
little." But while he may have confounded deep emotional intellectual
commitment to their religion with "emptiness," he saw that "they were the
fiercest element in the battle to establish a European life on the New
World. The first to come as a group, of a desire sprung within themselves,
they were the first American democracy. . . ."

Williams' treatment of the Pilgrims is certainly as harsh in places
as any anti-Puritan's could be. To him it seemed that they "instead of
growing, looked black at the world and damning its perfections praised a
zero in themselves. The inversion of a Gothic Calvin." His most militant assertions bear little relationship to the historical facts of their
existence or beliefs; but they give us some notion of the extent to which
Williams loathed all semblance of the "Puritan" mind: the prohibitionist,
the censor, all those who constrict or forbid. "This stress of the spirit
against the flesh has produced a race incapable of flower. Upon that part

of the earth they occupied true spirit dies because of the Puritans, except through vigorous revolt. They are the bane, not the staff. Their
religious zeal, mistaken for a thrust up toward the sun, was a stroke in,
in, in--not toward germination but the confinements of a tomb." The error in his equation of the original with the facsimile reproduction is
understandable in terms of the time at which In the American Grain was
conceived and written. To most artists and many others who should have
known better, the Puritans represented repressive and Philistine America.
Their militancy resulted in some great inaccuracies of vision, as Charles
Beard made clear in an article in The New Republic in 1920. "By the critics," he wrote, "[Puritanism] is used as a term of opprobrium applicable
to anything that interferes with the new freedom, free verse, psychoanal-
ysis, or even the double entendre."[20] When Williams writes that "it is
still to-day the Puritan who keeps his frightened grip upon the world
lest it should prove him--empty," he is confusing Puritan with what a
later generation with equal inaccuracy refers to as "the Establishment."

On the other hand Williams does portray with some feeling the toughness, bravery and loneliness of the Puritans. They certainly were not,
in their own minds, "without guidance," as he would have it; but they
were decidedly "in fear" much of the time and the hostility of their new
environment need never be underplayed. Their strength enabled them to
survive and yet Williams insists that the very foundation of their strength
was emptiness, and that their issue have mangled themselves and the continent they have settled. "The result of that brave setting out of the
Pilgrims has been an atavism that thwarts and destroys. The agonized
spirit, that has followed like an idiot with underdeveloped brain, governs

with its great muscles, babbling in a text of the dead years." His mis-
perception--his tracing of the atavism to the Winthrops, Bradfords and
Mathers rather than the Carnegies, Rockefellers and Sumners--is understandable. But granted that misperception the chapter is still a remarkable
piece of writing. It says still, for many Americans, what they feel they
know but cannot prove about the nature of their country.

What fascinates Williams most about Samuel de Champlain is a quality
that he never is quite able to put into words. Champlain, he writes, "_is_
a man after my own heart." But the reasons for this remain obscure unless
we know Williams well enough to reconstruct, outside the chapter itself,
the kind of personality he is trying to get across. He tells us, contra-
dicting Parkman, that far from being "'a man all for the theme and purpose,
nothing for himself'," Champlain was actually "a man all for himself--but
gently, with love, with patience, unwilling to endure the smallest fracture of his way of doing. He knew Champlain and followed Champlain in
everything." What he is talking about, as he hints later, is the same
kind of egoistic character traits he saw in Columbus the discoverer, coupled with a strong sense, in Champlain, of place and time and a vision
for the New World. But Champlain has a weakness that is not of the New
World and this in the end aligns him with the idealists rather than the
activists. His weakness is his distinctly European gentility and his determination to remain unruffled: "A short battle. Pont Gravé wounded.
This Basque with us has come to make a truce. Champlain was 'greatly annoyed,' his records say at such a beginning. Greatly annoyed! Isn't that
a treasure?"

However Champlain's great strength is his exactitude and this makes

him of value. He notes down and pictures all he sees. He measures and
surveys "the exact place where Jacques Cartier wintered formally" with
"fastidious pains . . . beyond the scientific possibility of a doubt."
He is like the doctor tracking down a disease or a fracture, or a poet
charting his way toward the most exact of utterances. He begins to emerge,
pulled as he is between adventure and meticulousness, as a kind of type
of Paterson himself. He is, like Williams behind the personality of his
greatest protagonist, at once the dreamer and creator of a city, "a man
absorbed in his work, eager, riding ahead of his plans." Faced with mutiny and quelling it he does not wish to punish, to take definable and
and understandable action, but like a doctor--or a writer--to find out
why the mutiny occurs. "Why have they wished to kill him, him Champlain?
He'd pardon every one, except those four [chief mutineers], if he could
learn the motive." Having traced the cause of the uprising, he finally
has only one man executed. Then he returns to Quebec.

At this point another voice, that of an unidentified second person
to whom Williams has addressed the entire chapter, breaks in to condemn
Champlain and the narrator's admiration for him. But this voice is also
Williams' own, the voice of the impatient, irascible American who cannot
see the value or the charm of Champlain's special qualities: "To hell
with all that: collecting pictures for France--or science--or art! A
spirit of resignation. Literature. Books--a library. Good night, then.
That's not you. YOU!" This is the voice of "rebellion, savagery; a force
to leap up and wrench you from your hold and force you to be part of it;
the place, the absolute new without a law but the basic blood where savage becomes brother." It breaks open Williams' mood--his revery over

Champlain--as it is later repeatedly to crash in upon Paterson as he sits in the library in the great poem of the later years. The key to Champlain's failure is that he could not break out into the spirit of the New World, as the narrator is forced to see. "The place . . . was outraged, that is-- if you are right--and I think you are. . . . He with his maps, for France, for science, for civilization. . . . I say it is marvelous--if you want it, but as against a New World--it is inconceivable."

The strange dialogue between Williams as a slightly European narrator who is delighted by Champlain's qualities and Williams the argumentative American ends with a broken paean from the latter voice: "The land! don't you feel it? Doesn't it make you want to go out and lift dead Indians tenderly from their graves, to steal from them--as if it must be clinging even to their corpses--some authenticity, that which--Here not there." This is confusing but ultimately effective. The interruption is provided by the calmer voice, finally convinced of the importance of that which makes a locality "here not there," that which makes America always America and never Europe. Finally, he sees it is that which caused Champlain to fail and makes him, despite his attention to detail and his course of benevolent self-interest, a figure who is never fully aligned with what is essentially American.

The chapter on "The May-Pole at Merry Mount" treats the story familiar to readers of Hawthorne or, more recently, Robert Lowell in a way entirely in keeping with Williams' hostility toward the Puritans.[21] But perhaps Williams makes more of Thomas Morton than he might, insisting that other historical accounts of the man have lacked "scale." Morton, for Williams, is above all else a "New World pioneer taking his chances in

the wilderness." He sees him as "unique in our history," primarily because Morton penetrated to the inherent sensuality of the New World by
consorting freely with its native inhabitants. Williams is at some pains
to "prove" the sexual license and provocative natures of Indian women.
Among other authorities he cites Francis Parkman's account of the Jesuit
missionary Le Jeune, whose life among the Algonquins must have been, at
the least, offensive to his sensibilities. "Le Jeune says, 'Les filles
et les jeunes femmes sont a l'exterieur très honnestement couvertes, mais
entre elles leurs discours sont puants, commes des cloaques.'"

Williams excuses Morton's dealing in alcohol and guns, refusing to
acknowledge the incendiary nature of such actions: "since the whites were
armed with guns and had liquor, was it in the eyes of history wrong for
Morton to use them for his trade?" This of course evades what was for the
Puritans the real point about Morton's misconduct. The attack was made
in the name of moral decency but the thrust of the anger was against Morton
as a threat to the whole society not Morton as an immoral pest. As Williams
notes later in the chapter, they also had "the trade in beaver skins in
view." It was not, as Williams insists, that the Puritans "lacked spirit
to explain" Morton's licentious and inflammatory behavior; it was rather
that it was only too explicable to their religious outlook and in conflict
with their economic self-interest.

The chapter on Merry Mount, originally Ma-re Mount from the Indian,
now Mount Wollaston, near Wollaston, Massachusetts, is a lead-in for Williams' presentation of selections from Cotton Mather's "Wonders of the
Invisible World." Since he presents Mather's words without editorial comment, he has to get his point about the Puritans across in the chapters

on the Mayflower's voyage and the Morton affair. In the "Voyage" he refers directly to the Mather chapter once and talks again about the Puritans' behavior at Salem. "In fear and without guidance, really lost in
the world, it is they alone who would later, at Salem, have strayed so
far--morbidly seeking the flame,--that terrifying unknown image to which,
like savages, they too offered sacrifices of human flesh." The Merry
Mount chapter ends with the clear indication that the Salem catastrophe
is for Williams the center-piece of his presentation of Puritan culture:
"Trustless of humane experience, not knowing what to think, they went mad,
lost all direction. Mather defends the witchcraft persecutions."

The selection from Mather can hardly be faulted from the point of
view of presenting one coherent vision of Puritan life. But there is little indication in what Williams selects of Mather's largeness of vision
or concern as a leader and thinker for his community. Almost all of the
chapter is comprised of the trials of Bridget Bishop and Susanna Martin
at Salem in June of 1692. Appended are two "curiosities" which Mather
presented, in good faith, in order that "if there be found any mistake,
it may be willingly Retracted, as it was unwillingly Committed." Williams
probably included Mather's short preface to add an ironic twist to the
inhumanity of the trials. He clearly thought that Mather himself could
express the perverse nature of the Puritan experience more effectively
than anything he himself might write. It is a successful experiment for
his purposes and one which he was to employ extensively again to capture
and present other personalities and events in Paterson.

If the selections from Mather, prefaced by references in the Mayflower and Morton chapters are effective in putting across Williams' attitudes

toward the Puritans, the real tour de force of Puritan-gouging, and in
some ways the most important and impressive piece of writing in In the
American Grain, is the essay on Père Sebastian Rasles. Williams evidently at least started it while he was in Europe, after his first visit to
Paris, while in the South of France, Rome and Vienna.[22]

The chapter opens with a catalog of the people he had met on his
first 1924 visit to Paris in their, to him, most characteristic poses or
dress: "Picasso (turning to look back, with a smile), Braque (brown cotton), Gertrude Stein (opening the doors of a cabinet of MSS.), Tzara
(grinning), . . . Jámes and Norah Joyce (in a taxi at the Place de l'É-
toile), McAlmon, Antheil, Bryher, H. D. and dear Ezra who took me to talk
with Léger; and finally Adrienne Monnier--those were my six weeks in Paris."
He characterizes himself at the time as well, "with antennae fully extended, but nothing came of it save an awakened realization within myself of that resistant core of nature upon which I had so long been driv-
en for support." It was Adrienne Monnier, however, Sylvia Beach's friend
and colleague, who brought Williams one of his "best moments among those
days of rushing about and talking and seeing," by introducing him to
Valéry Larbaud, the eminently sophisticated and cosmopolitan historian,
writer and translator. Out of that meeting grew this chapter and a conversation between the two men forms its framework.

Williams portrays himself as apprehensive about meeting Larbaud,
crouched in the defensive, counter-intellectual posture that produced
so many of his thorniest utterances in those years. "Who is this man
Larbaud who has so little pride that he wishes to talk with me? . . .

He is a student, I am a block, I thought. I could see it at once: he
knows far more of what is written of my world than I. But he is a student while I am--the brutal thing itself." But despite Williams' worst
fears the afternoon of conversation was a rich and rewarding one for him.
He wrote twice of it to Marianne Moore during the ensuing weeks, first on
February 21st to report that "I had a fine afternoon alone with Valéry
Larbaud, who talked to me of Spanish literature, giving me ten names
(enclosed) of the newer men. We also talked of Bolivar and the grand manner in which Spain undertook its new world colonization as contrasted with
England's niggardliness. We spoke also of Cotton Mather!!"[23] Later on, in
April, Williams mentions Larbaud to Miss Moore again: "Valéry Larbaud
spoke only of Bolivar's sweep of imagination. The English came to America on a 3% basis, but Bolivar saw another Spain in America. He liked
the way the Spaniards 'moved in' to the new world, bringing lares, penates
and Olympus too with them. I could say little at the sight of the six
two-inch-thick volumes on Bolivar which Larbaud threw before me, like pome-
granates, on the table. Perhaps I stammered a word about admiring something of the Maya cultures."[24]

As the chapter progresses the conversation develops. Williams remains
at his most defensive: "He presumed too much. I am not a student; presently he will ask me questions I cannot answer!" This personal sense of
inferiority grows to include America itself. "We are none. Who are we?
Degraded whites riding our fears to market where everything is by accident
and only one thing sure: the fatter we get the duller we grow; only a
simpering disgust . . . reveals any contact with a possible freshness--
and that only by inversion." This outburst is something of a momentary

purgation of the frustration and impatience of the early Twenties for Williams, and in conversation with this extraordinary teacher he gradually begins to move toward a real statement of substance, one which lies at the very heart of his intentions in In the American Grain:

> We have no books, I said.
> There you are wrong. Two or three are
> enough, to have shown a beginning. Have
> you not yourself proven that there is meat----
> Yes (so he had read what I intended!),
> the early records--to try to find--something,
> a freshness; if it exist.
> I said, It is an extraordinary phenom-
> enon that Americans have lost the sense, be-
> ing made up as we are, that what we are has
> its origin in what the nation in the past
> has been; that there is a source IN AMERICA
> for everything we think or do; that morals
> affect the food and food the bone, and that,
> in fine, we have no conception at all of what
> is meant by moral, since we recognize no ground
> our own--and that this rudeness rests all up-
> on the unstudied character of our beginnings;
> and that if we will not pay heed to our own
> affairs, we are nothing but an unconscious
> porkyard and oilhole for those, more able,
> who will fasten themselves upon us. And that
> we have no defense, lacking intelligent in-
> vestigation of the changes worked upon the
> early comers here, to the New World, the books,
> the records, no defense save brute isolation,
> prohibitions, walls, ships, fortresses--and
> all the asininities of ignorant fear that for-
> bids us to protect a doubtful freedom by em-
> ploying it. That unless everything that is,
> proclaim a ground on which it stand, it has
> no worth; and that what has been morally, aes-
> thetically worth while in America has rested
> upon peculiar and discoverable ground. But
> they think they get it out of the air or the
> rivers, or from the Grand Banks or wherever
> it may be, instead of by word of mouth or from
> records contained for us in books--and that
> aesthetically, morally we are deformed unless
> we read.

Larbaud's response is to mention Mather's Magnalia. And this at once

thrills and agonizes Williams because while it is precisely one of the
books he has had in mind he feels that Larbaud's acquaintance with it
is greater than his own: "HE had read it. I had seen the book and brushed
through its pages hunting for something I wished to verify. Un grand
prédicateur." Williams goes on to say to Larbaud that he had found Mather
"tiresome," and Larbaud agrees but calls Mather "very strong, very real."
There then ensues a conversation on the Puritans in which all Williams'
previous assumptions--those in the earlier two chapters of his own and the
selections from Mather he chose as exemplary--are put unabashedly to the
test. Larbaud admits to a certain grotesquerie in the Puritan religion,
but finds it "firm . . . solid, it holds the understanding in its true
position . . . like science at its best. . . . There is vigor there--
and by that, a beauty."

Williams argues back against this, admitting vigor, but dwelling
again on the smallness and narrowness of the Puritans, the atrophy of
their vision and their crippling impact on the New World and themselves:
"There it is, concise, bare, PURE: blind to every contingency, mashing
Indian, child and matron into one safe mold." He continues, adding that
the Puritans "closed all the world out. . . . All that they saw they
lived by but denied. And this is overlooked." Larbaud breaks in to ask
why Americans do not speak more often of such things as the persecution
of the early Quakers in New England and Williams answers, "Because the
fools do not believe that they have sprung from anything. . . . They
float without question. Their history is to them an enigma."

Larbaud defends the founders of America, insisting in remarkably
Freudian terms that "As with all histories, it begins with giants--cruel,

but enormous, who eat flesh. They were giants." Then he requests that
Williams distinguish between "the rugged English pioneers and a theoret-
ic dogma that clung to them unevenly." Williams remains firm and declares
that there is "a 'puritanism'--of which you hear, of course, but you have
never felt it stinking all about you--that has survived to us from the
past." Larbaud continues to test and to goad, and Williams' handling of
the dialogue is as dramatically sure as if he had had a tape recorder from
which to transcribe and translate the encounter verbatim:

> Proceed. Mather. What a force, still to
> interest you; it is admirable. But I find
> your interest "très théorique."
> What! I cried. Wait a bit. These men
> are not the only ones of these times.
> It is of books that we were speaking.
> It is of books that I wish to tell you.
> Then they live still, those books?
> I could not assure him that they did,
> those books of Mather's. As books, no, I
> said to him. But what is in them lives and
> there hides, as in a lair from whence it sal-
> lies now and then to strike terror through
> the land.
> And you would be the St. George? Are they
> then in such a bad state in America, in such
> a swamp? I thought--
> As always, I answered him. This fiery
> breath, as of a dragon, is to us a living
> thing. Our resistance to the wilderness has
> been too strong. It has turned us anti-Amer-
> ican, anti-literature. As a violent "puri-
> tanism" it breathes. Still. In these books
> is its seed.

From this exchange, egged on by Larbaud, Williams moves into his
story of Père Rasles, whose greatest single quality is his lack of "resistance to the wilderness." Rasles' character, as Williams sees him, is
deeply sensual and in tune with the environment. He seems "a spirit, rich,
blossoming, generous, able to give and to receive, full of taste, a nose,

a tongue, a laugh, enduring, self-forgetful in benificence--a new spirit
in the New World." Rasles is, in short, a seventeenth-century paragon of
those qualities Williams himself had been championing since his first serious attempts to write and to understand America.

The story of Rasles and his "cher troupeau" takes over from the conversation between Williams and Larbaud and Williams tells it with economy
and emphasis, quoting from Rasles' Lettres Édifiantes to prove in as many
ways as possible that "Contrary to the English, Rasles recognized the New
World." His gift was his ability to "touch" the environment and its inhabitants, to live their lives and bring his all-encompassing religion a-
mong them. Williams concludes his brief biography with the assertion that
"the average American [is] an Indian, but an Indian robbed of his world----
unless we call machines a forest in themselves." His corollary is that
the average American, despite his Protestant background, is drifting
towards Catholicism, which explains "the growth of the Catholic Church
with us today"; and that what has caused that growth is the "lack of
touch" of Puritanism. "From lack of touch," Williams argues, "lack of
belief. Steadily the individual loses caste, then the local government
loses its authority; the head is more and more removed. Finally the center is reached----totally dehumanized, like a Protestant heaven. Everything is Federalized and all laws become prohibitive in essence." The
Church, Williams feels, "offers to a headless mob a government, and THAT
is its appeal (to take immediately the place of that lost local one that
used to touch.)"

While Williams' synthesis of the American situation savors of late

afternoon euphoria, his sentiments here are a far cry from the anti-Cathol-
icism of his improvisation, "The Little Polish Father of Kingsland." The
basic commitment, however, remains the same. He is against sterility and
regimentation, just as he was in his earlier writing; and he is for a force
which will bring contact with the real into peoples' lives. The great difference is that to the writer of Kora in Hell it often seemed that only the
imagination could provide that "touch." By the time he came to write In
the American Grain, Williams was fully aware that there is a certain way
to live one's life as an American which will keep one "in touch" with both
past and present. The afternoon conversation with Valéry Larbaud seems
to have had the key importance of crystallizing Williams' convictions and
making him increasingly confident of their viability.

Another man who, like Rasles, lived by his senses and respected rather than feared the great wilderness was Daniel Boone. In the opening of
his chapter on Boone, Williams calls him "a great voluptuary . . . full
of a rich regenerative violence." But his essay on him qualifies this
and makes of him a very specific kind of "voluptuary"--one, like Rasles,
whose chief gratification is harmony with nature. The "violence" of the
man is the violence of the solitary giver and taker. There is nothing
gratuitous about it: "Mild and simple hearted, steady, not impulsive in
courage--bold and determined, but always rather inclined to defend than
attack--he stood immensely above that wretched class of men who are so often the preliminaries of civilization."

Williams' source for the Boone chapter was "the so-called autobiography, said to have been written down from Boone's dictation, late in his
life by one John Filson." While he is impatient with "the silly phrases

and total disregard for what must have been the rude words of the old hunter" he finds in the Filson rendition, Williams' own diction is occasionally almost as much of another century. Describing Boone's early manhood on the Yadkin River and the gradual growth of the population there, Williams writes, "These accessions of companionship, however congenial to the greatest part of mankind, did not suit Boone." The sentence might have come from The Lives of the Poets. But his vision of Boone pierces through Filson's version of the life. His own sympathetic grasp of the man makes him exclaim that "When Filson goes on to declare Boone's loneliness 'an uninterupted scene of sylvan pleasures' it is a little too much to bear. Constant exposure to danger and death, a habitation which he states had been discovered by the savages, the necessity of such strategems as the resort to the canebrake rather than to take the risk of being found in his cabin, have nothing of sylvan pleasures in them."

One extremely important phrase, the parent of a concept that lies close to the center of Paterson, comes to first light in this chapter. "Not that he settled Kentucky or made a path to the west," writes Williams of Boone, "not that he defended, suffered, hated and fled, but because of a descent to the ground of his desire was Boone's life important and does it remain still loaded with power,--power to strengthen every form of energy that would be voluptuous, passionate, possessive in that place which he opened." (Italics mine.)

Boone is indeed "a lineal descendant of Columbus on the beach at Santo Domingo" to Williams, but he is a lineal descendant of that Columbus only, before the decline in fortunes which followed his greatest moment. Boone has no patterns of life that are foreign to his environment to trammel him. As Williams sees him, Boone is the exemplar of the white man coming to terms with a new continent: "Boone stood for his race, the affirmation of that wild logic, which in times past had mastered another wilderness and now, renascent, would master this, to prove it potent." His is not to be the role of the Indian, though he must in many ways resemble him. Rather he must be "himself in a new world, Indian-like." At the opposite end of the scale from the Puritans, Boone sees the Indian not as an "aberrant type, treacherous and anti-white to be feared and exterminated, but as a natural expression of the place, the Indian himself as 'right,' the flower of his world." Even the murder of his eldest son by Indians generates in Boone "no illwill against the Red Men."

Unlike Columbus, Boone held out successfully against the major competitive power in his world--the Federalization of Hamilton's America. To Williams he remained to the end "the antagonist of those of his own blood whose alien strength he felt and detested, while his whole soul, with greatest devotion, was given to the New World which he adored and found, in its every expression, the land of heart's desire." It is important to stress that Williams does not see Boone as a man more primitive than his fellows, but as one better able to adapt to the essential nature of the place in which he lived. Here he found a man, like Rasles, who had made and held contact with his environment. Boone really stands alone in In the American Grain, for of all the Americans he is the one who remains at once truest to his vision and closest to the land from which that vision was gained.[25]

The quality Williams singles out as the "actual peculiarity" in George Washington's character is his "resistance" to the raging compulsions inside and outside himself. "Resistance was, I believe, his code," writes Williams. Encitadeled. A protector of the peace, or at least, keeper of the stillness within himself." He pictures Washington in one superb paragraph in a way thoroughly alien to the figure who rides solumnly across the Delaware in many grade school classrooms in America:

> Here was a man of tremendous vitality buried in a massive frame and under a rather stolid and untractable exterior which the ladies somewhat feared, I fancy. He must have looked well to them, from a distance, or say on horseback--but later it proved a little too powerful for comfort. And he wanted them too; violently. One can imagine him curiously alive to the need of dainty waistcoats, lace and kid gloves, in which to cover that dangerous rudeness which he must have felt about himself. His interest in dress at a certain period of his career is notorious.

In a curious way Washington reminds us, in this brief portrait, of Williams as he saw himself from time to time. Like Washington, Williams was a man who depended on "peace and regularity" although he had the ability to endure stress. Control of internal and external realities to avoid stress and conflict mark the lives of both men. Williams made art of his obsessions and compulsions; Washington achieved military and political greatness by translating the "hell fire" Williams saw raging inside the man into a resistless implacability. As Williams notes in a particularly acute piece of psychological perception, men like Washington who suffer-- or achieve--"a political conversion of their emotions" are "always the noteworthy among us. Battle to them must be the expression of that something in themselves which they fear. Washington's calmness of demeanor and characteristics as a military leader were of that cloth."

Yet despite Washington's control, Williams finds him ultimately a

"sacrifice to the mob--in a great many ways thoroughly disappointing."
Men like Washington--"great wench lovers" whose ambitions are limited by
the amount of personal control they exercise--suffer the same fate as in-
novative artists whose efforts are swept aside by changes in public taste.
"The whole crawling mass gnaws on them--hates them," writes Williams in
an undemocratic outburst. "He was hated, don't imagine he was not. The
minute he had secured their dung heap for them--he had to take their dirt
in the face." Perhaps some of this ambivalence toward Washington is rooted
in Williams' own experiences as a writer: in the collapse of Contact and
the overwhelming pre-eminence of Eliot on the literary scene.

Williams' chapter on Ben Franklin, "Poor Richard," is comprised of
two sections. The first, "Information to Those Who Would Remove to America," like the Mather chapter, is verbatim material from the subject himself. The second section, "Notes for a Commentary on Franklin," is a serious effort to define the man's failure in terms of his great potential
as an inhabitant of the New World.

Franklin, as Williams sees him, was possessed of a quality similar
to the "great voluptuary," Boone. Williams calls it "the sheer mass of
his voluptuous energy . . . a trait he borrowed without recognition from
the primitive profusion of his surroundings." But unlike Boone, Franklin was afraid of that energy and of its source. While granting him
strength and vigor, Williams observes that Franklin, unlike his continent,
was "without beauty." He observes that "The force of the New World is
never in [such] men open; it is sly, covert, almost cringing." Franklin's
identifying characteristic is his "touching" things, but his touch is a

very different sort from Boone's or Rasles' formidable contact with the
elemental force of the new. "The terrible beauty of the New World at-
tracts men to their ruin," writes Williams, and indeed he had showed this
with his treatment of Columbus and de Soto most especially. "Franklin
did not care to be ruined--he only wanted to touch."

As a representative of his time and his world--as an American--Frank-
lin is far from being unusual in Williams' mind. There is just more of
him: more power and more opportunity at a decisive historical moment.
But Williams is frank to admit that there "has not yet appeared in the
New World any one with sufficient strength for the open assertion; . . .
it is necessary to Boone to lose himself in the wilds; . . . Houston's
bride is frightened off; the New Englanders are the clever bone-men. Nowhere the open, free assertion save in the Indian: this is the quality."
One has the distinct impression that at the back of Williams' mind is the
desire to make that "open assertion" with his own life and work, and with
In the American Grain in particular.

As with Washington, there is the suggestion of enormous sexual drives
behind Franklin's vitality:

> His fingers itched to be meddling, to do the
> little concrete thing--the barrier against
> a flood of lightning that would inundate him. . . .
> Fear drove his curiosity.
> Do something, anything, to keep his fin-
> gers busy--not to realize--the lightning. Be
> industrious, let money and comfort increase;
> money is like a bell that keeps the dance
> from terrifying, as it would if it were silent
> and we could hear the grunt,--thud--swish.

In Williams' mind these drives are associated with the New World itself
and with the greatest powers of Nature--the lightning that Franklin "had

to fool with," because "he didn't dare let it go in at the top of his head
and out at his toes."

Interestingly enough, nowhere in his "Notes for a Commentary" does
Williams associate Franklin with the Puritan tradition: an indication,
perhaps, of a lack of coherence in his historical view of the seventeenth
and eighteenth centuries. The material for such an association is certainly there, but Williams does not seem to want to tie Franklin into a clas-
sification which by his definition excluded men of such engrossing energy.
He sees that "The nation was the offspring of the desire to huddle, to
protect--of terror"; and that our "pioneer statesmen" gave "their fine energy, as they must have done, to the smaller, narrower, protective thing
and not to the great, New World." But he is either reluctant or oblivious
of the chance to relate the behavior of the Pilgrim Fathers to the Fathers
of the Country. He seems to have seen the two most important factors in
the shape of our society as separate and distinct rather than as part of
an historical continuum.

For his chapter on John Paul Jones, Williams chose to reproduce in
toto a letter from Jones to Franklin written on board the Serapis on October 3, 1779, several days after the defeat and capture of that ship by
Jones on September 23rd. The "odd note" about the battle that Williams
mentions in his original jacket statement seems to be Jones' fury at his
allied commanders. What comes through in Jones' letter is the incompe-
tence and indeed the treachery of the other captains in his fleet, especially one Captain Landais. Jones alone appears to be concerned with the
cause of the Revolution, and he observes that the majority of the others
"have appeared bent on the pursuit of interest only." Williams seems to

have felt that in the understatement of Jones' style, the sustained tone
of suppressed excitement in battle and suppressed rage at the conduct of
the others involved, he had the real qualities of the man available. To
comment further on Jones would have violated the portrait presented by
the man himself.

In his chapter "Jacataqua," however, Williams made no effort to curb
his editorializing. The result is several poorly organized pages of commentary on America in general and the American woman in particular. The
angry voice of the editor of Contact surges through the section, and the
coherence of other chapters is sacrificed to high feeling.

He makes an opening assertion that "terror enlarges the object, as
does joy," and proceeds to attack the balance of the two elements in our
folklore and legend. He points out that while there is ample evidence of
"a great dread" in our past, "there is rarely a countering legend of joy."
He continues, "We believe that life in America is compact of violence and
the shock of immediacy. This is not so. Were it so, there would be a
corresponding beauty of the spirit--to bear it witness; a great flowering,
simple and ungovernable as the configuration of a rose--that should stand
with the gifts of the spirit of other times and other nations as a standard to humanity. There is none." The reason for this, in Williams' scheme
of things, is our fear: a fear inherited from the Puritans and their direct descendants. Other countries have possibilities of getting beyond
experience to wisdom, as Freud showed, "Jenseits des lust princip," or
as Williams paraphrases him, "beyond the charmed circle." But in America
we are governed by our fear of experience, of contact and, following Franklin, of touch: "Here, through terror, there is no direct touch; all is

cold, little and discreet: --save just under the hide." Williams finds

us "deanimated," and he abhors our love of violence, though he sees even

that love tempered by indirection. We forestall continually "the impact

of the bare soul upon the very twist of the fact which is our world about

us."

The result of this lack of genuine passion, and the surest symptom

of the emptiness of our culture is that we have never seen "a true woman

in flower." "Emily Dickinson," writes Williams, "starving of passion in

her father's garden, is the very nearest we have ever been--starving."

He carries his assertion a step further, bringing women and poets togeth-

er by a peculiar leap of logic: "Never a woman: never a poet. That's

an axiom. Never a poet saw sun here."

After several rather muddled pages in which he attempts to analyze

various aspects of American womanhood as it is crushed and snuffed out

by our culture, Williams returns to the parallel between poets and women

in a particularly knotty and confusing paragraph:

> Poets, through their energy, receive such
> a stamp of the age upon their work, that they
> are marked, in fact, even in the necessities
> of their defeat, as having lived well in their
> time. Poets are defeated but in an essential
> and total defeat at any time, that time is
> stamped in character upon their work, they give
> shape to the formless age as by a curious die,
> --and so other times recognize them, the pos-
> itives that created the forms which give char-
> acter and dignity to the damp mass of the over-
> powering but characterless resistance. So
> Jacataqua gave to womanhood in her time, the
> form which bitterness of pioneer character had
> denied it.

What Williams says here is only incidentally concerned with women, de-

spite the fact that the passage serves as a lead-in to the short scene

in which Jacataqua finally appears in the chapter bearing her name. This
is really a crucial statement by a poet about his role as he sees it in
relation to his times. Like some of the more bewildering moments in Spring
and All, the statement as Williams has made it requires a virtual translation: as if the man's prose had been warped into incomprehensibility by
the weight of the utterance he is making. Even as they are subdued by
their age, Williams seems to be saying, poets are among the leading expo-
nents of that age. They are men who have lived "well," in the sense of
"fully," "in their time." History--the raw material of events and personality in a society--is "the damp mass of the overpowering but character-
less resistance" that at once overwhelms the poet but is given "character
and dignity" by him. In recording his tribulations and defeat, the work
of the poet becomes, like a "die" or casting mold, a definition, limita-
tion, and shaper of an otherwise "formless age."

The analogy of Jacataqua is a false one because Williams makes of her
the romantic incarnation of all that has been denied American women rather than the recorder, in her "defeat," of the actuality. She becomes a
sort of New World Diana, challenging Burr to hunt: "'These,' with a wave
of her brown hand toward Howard and the group of officers, 'these want
meat. You hunt with me? I win.'" The great problem with this chapter
is that Williams' connection between poets and women does not hold in the
terms in which he presents it, and the figure of Jacataqua has little of
the quality of definition he posits for poetry.

By his own account, it was his wife who did the research and reading for Williams' chapter on Aaron Burr. He titled it ironically "The
Virtue of History," for the chief aim of the piece is passionately to dis-

pute the common historical view of Burr as "a frightful danger to the
young state" who "needed to be curbed." The chapter is written as a dialogue between a defender of the traditional view of Burr and a rebellious
devotee of the man's freedom and strength. But the underlying dichotomy
is really between history and literature--between standard historical treat-
ments, in short, and the kind of lively impressionistic writing that was
Williams' own approach in In the American Grain. "History," states the
freer spirit of the two, "follows governments and never men. It portrays
us in generic patterns, like effigies or the carvings on sarcophagi, which
say nothing save, of such and such a man, that he is dead. That's history."
Against the cold recording and paralyzing qualities of history stands "the
stylist" who creates "literature, in which alone humanity is protected a-
gainst tyrannous design." This rebellious voice, which we must infer is
closest to the author's own, does not dismiss the historian's craft altogether by any means; he rather deplores its misuse. "History that should
be a left hand to us, as of a violinist, we bind up with prejudice, warp-
ing it to suit our fears as Chinese women do their feet." To counteract
this deformation, the voice continues, we must first assume that "no opinion can be trusted; even the facts may be nothing but a printer's error;
but if a verdict be unanimous, it is sure to be a wrong one. . . . If
we cannot make a man live again when he is gone, it is boorish to impris-
on him dead within some narrow definition, when, were he in his shoes before us, we could not do it. It's lies, such history, and dangerous."
In this assertion there is contained the kernel of the intention behind
Williams' aim in In the American Grain: it is precisely his desire to
"make a man live again" that impels him to write most of the chapters of

the book itself.

To treat Burr fairly means, to the anti-traditionalist, taking "the whole period" at which he lived and examining it "not as history, that lie! but as a living thing, something moving, undecided, swaying." The period of the Revolution is to be seen as one characterized by "freedom of conscience, a new start . . . quit of Europe." Against this freedom, to Burr and his defender, are ranged the Federalists: "Hamilton . . . the Federalist champion" and "Washington, as President, 'a monster of prudence,' . . . the helpless mother." The voice of the traditionalist breaks in after a particularly harsh denunciation of Hamilton with a well-deserved cautionary note: "You violate your own concept of what history should be when you speak so violently." The retort is logically weak but rhetorically effective: "The pendulum must swing. Is it not time that it swing back?" Throughout the remainder of the chapter the great bulk of the conversation is carried by Burr's defender. Few of the man's faults or vices are overlooked, but they are all seen as aspects of his great vitality and freedom. His legendary love of women and fathering of "an hundred bastard children" are viewed as evidence that Burr had kept the personal liberty that others had given up "for the general good." At one point the pro-Burr voice declares, "He's in myself and so I dig through lies to resurrect him," and indeed the historical figure of the man begins to take on certain characteristics familiar to the readers of Williams' own work. Burr is seen as a man "who believed in himself and his teaching and his blood." His licentiousness is seen against the background of sensual indulgence which marks many of Williams' favorite figures from "La Grosse Margot" to Père Rasles. "The world," declares the anti-traditionalist,

"is made to eat, not leave, that the spirit may be full, not empty. . . .
Burr knew what a democracy must liberate. . . . Men intact--with all
their senses waking. He had, raised to a different level, the directness
of 'common people' which reformers, that is to say, schemers, commonly
neglect, misname, misapprehend, as if it were anything but to touch, to
hear, to see, to smell, to taste." As an illustration of the "directness
of the 'common people,'" the voice produces a recollection which could
have been straight out of one of the improvisations or short stories: "A
while ago, just here, I heard a Polish woman saying to her daughter: 'You
bust your coat with your fifty sweaters.'" The ensuing clarification of
the value of such language reads like a defense of Williams' own best art.
The voice praises the Polish woman's remark, noting

> its immediacy, its sensual quality, a pure
> observation, its lack of irritation, its
> lack of pretense, its playful exaggeration,
> its repose, its sense of design, its open-
> ness, its gayety, its unconstraint. It frees,
> it creates relief. In the great it is the
> same, or would be if ever it existed, a deli-
> cious sincerity (in greater things of course)
> not a scheme, nor a system of procedure--but
> careless truth. . . . Burr's life was of
> that stuff. It is this that is trying to
> escape in a democracy.

As the pro-Burr voice, the Williams voice, has said earlier, "He is in
me. . . ." The qualities in Burr that Williams lauds in this chapter are
precisely the ones which were of vital importance to his own life and art.

"The Advent of the Slaves" is perhaps the least successful chapter
in In the American Grain because it completely fails to come to terms with
the American Negro. Throughout its few short paragraphs Williams struggles to assign to the Black man an essential quality. What he comes up

with is symptomatic of generational blindness, and his perception is not
remotely comparable to the keen grasp of the other sections of the book.
His admiration admittedly goes beyond the stock delight in "dancing, sing-
ing with the wild abandon of being close . . . waggin', wavin', weavin',
shakin'," though rhythm and carefreeness in the Black man are paid some
nodding obeisance. What Williams seizes upon as most characteristic of
the Negro is his "nothingness," and this is a difficult quality to express
with respect. To his credit, he is entirely open about his feelings; but
he shares with his age, in this chapter, a notion of the Black race that
reflects the deepest kind of blindness and prejudice. "There is a solidity," he writes, "a racial irreducible minimum, which gives them poise in
a world where they have no authority--." It was not until Williams, as
Paterson, forced himself to face his own ambivalence toward Blacks and
especially Black women, that he began to deal satisfactorily with his
prejudice as a writer.[27] In this chapter, at the best, he displays a keen
eye and ear for dialogue. But his delight in the ability of the Negro to
be a "nobody" does him no credit and it is startingly at odds with his
deeply compassionate attitude towards those disadvantaged by history or
by "progress" elsewhere in In the American Grain.

Sam Houston's "descent" to primitive life with the Cherokees becomes
in the chapter, "Descent," a metaphor for the route the American artist
must follow to get back to his native tradition. The first paragraph of
this short section is, suitably enough, an amalgam of biographical data
on Houston and a pronouncement on "the primitive destiny of the land"
which sounds very much like a Contact editorial. Throughout the chapter
Williams shifts easily back and forth between Houston's life and the state

of American letters. Houston, Poe and Whitman are all seen by Williams
as men who have rooted down into themselves and the ground they live on,
as was Boone in "The Discovery of Kentucky." Both the hero of the Alamo
and the American poet who would do something for and out of his native
culture "must penetrate" the "stratum of obscurity" that is comprised of
"a field of unrelated culture stuccoed" over the real "primitive destiny
of the land." There is about Houston's life a certain "aesthetic satisfaction," as there is about all the subjects Williams treats in In the
American Grain. This satisfaction is the basis of the poet's craft and
Williams sees it being denied by the American civilization with its over-
lay of cultures not native to its own soil. In applying Houston's "descent" to his own time and avocation, Williams writes, "A poet is one related to a basis of material, aesthetic, spiritual, hypothetical, abnor-
mal--satisfaction." The need for this satisfaction "goes for the most
part unsatisfied in America or is satisfied by a fillgap. The predomi-
nant picture of America is a land aesthetically satisfied by temporary
fillgaps. But the danger remains: Taste is so debauched in the end that
everything of [the] new will be forgotten and--."

Williams continues his highly effective vacillation between Houston
and literature and along the way he gets into the familiar defensive posture vis-a-vis those who, like Eliot and Pound, have not "descended" but
rather transferred the loci of their cultural attentions.

> It is imperative that we sink. But from
> a low position it is impossible to answer
> those who know all the Latin and some of the
> Sanskrit names, much French and perhaps one
> or two other literatures. Their riposte is:
> Knownothingism. But we cannot climb every
> tree in that world of birds. But where for-

> eign values are held to be a desideratum, he
> who is burned and speaks thickly--is lost.
>   There is nothing for a man but genius or
> despair. We cannot answer in the smart lan-
> guage, certainly it would be a bastardization
> of our own talents to waste time to learn the
> language they use. I would rather sneak off
> and die like a sick dog than be a well known
> literary person in America--and no doubt I'll
> do it in the end. Our betters we may bitter-
> ly advise: Know nothing (i.e., the man on
> the street), make no attempt to know. With a
> foreign congeries of literary clap-trap, come
> without courtesy to a strange country and make
> for yourself a smooth track to the pockets of
> the mob by catering to a 'refined' taste and
> soiling that which you do not know how to es-
> timate. Courtesy would at least bid him be
> informed or keep still. . . .

Just who the suddenly introduced third person "him" is at the end is impossible to guess. Certainly the references to Sanskrit and French point
to Eliot, yet the coming to a "strange country" sounds rather as though
Williams is referring in passing to someone who has arrived in America
and has written about it without knowing anything or anyone, "i.e., the
man on the street."

The chapter ends with a statement reminiscent of several in Spring
and All: "However hopeless it may seem, we have no other choice: we must
go back to the beginning; it must all be done over; everything that is
must be destroyed." But we must understand this in the context of the
chapter in which it appears. It is not total destruction Williams is calling for but a rejection of the worst and the most misleading elements in
our cultural tradition. What he seeks here is the going to ground, like
Houston, to refresh one's vision and make contact with the most basic realities of the American experience.

From the point of view of clarifying Williams' feelings about the

role of the American artist, the most important single chapter in <u>In the</u>
<u>American Grain</u> is "Edgar Allan Poe." To Williams, Poe represented the
first truly American writer, not in the sense of "nationality in letters,"
but rather in that he was "the astounding, inconceivable growth of his
locality." In other words the fact that Poe was American by birth is not
as important as that he created an American art by remaining true to his
locale by means both of the style and the content of his writing.

In <u>The Great American Novel</u>, Williams had noted that "representative
American verse will be that which will appear new to the French . . . prose
the same." Poe's influence on the French, as Williams points out in the
opening of the chapter, is due to his "scrupulous originality, <u>not</u> 'originality' in the bastard sense, but in its legitimate sense of solidity
which goes back to the ground, a conviction that he <u>can</u> judge within himself. These things the French were <u>ready</u> to perceive and quick to use to
their advantage. . . ." In Poe's work "colonial imitation" and "courtesy"
are abandoned in favor of "a fresh beginning" and "truth." Like Boone the
settler or Houston the Indian-lover, Poe's artistic direction is a "descent" to the roots of American reality. His critical writing is "a movement, first and last, to clear the GROUND."

James Guimond writes that "Poe is the consummate American idealist
in <u>In the American Grain</u>--and the one Williams considered most relevant
to contemporary American conditions."[28] But there is a sense in which Poe
achieves his goals as an artist, despite his premature and lonely death,
in a way that makes him less of an "idealist," in Guimond's terms, than,
say, Columbus. Poe was, to Williams, the agent of "the first great burst
through to expression of a re-awakened genius of <u>place</u>." Unlike Columbus,

Poe was very much aware of his agency as an innovator and also very much in touch with his subject-matter and voice as an artistic and critical exponent of the New World.

One recalls Williams' essay on "America, Whitman and the Art of Poetry" in 1917, in which he praised Whitman for destroying "the forms antiquity decreed him to take and use." In his art Whitman "started again naked but built not very far." Poe also goes back to the beginning of things, dealing, however, not so much with new forms as with new material, the material dictated by his presence in a new locale. In doing so he brings to America and the world a literature born of his singularly novel blend of imagination and logic. "His attack was _from the center out_," writes Williams. That is his identity, time and place directed him to wage war on existing conventions and on their devotees and practitioners not as an "outsider" but as an American more native and truer to his environment than Longfellow or Lowell. The New World for Poe the artist as for Williams almost a hundred years later "must be mine as I will have it, or it is a worthless bog. There can be no concession."

Williams twice quotes Poe's statement in "Mr. Griswold and the Poets" that "the highest order of the imaginative intellect is always preeminently mathematical." He goes on to quote a passage from the same essay that sounds very much like his own observations in "Yours, O Youth," an essay in _Contact_ 3 discussed earlier. In it Williams had written:

> The few among us who might write well in any generation, however they will be trained, fear to believe that in writing it will be exactly as it has been in other spheres of inventive activity, that the project has not grown until precedent has been rendered secondary to necessity or completely ignored.

> It has been by paying naked attention first
> to the thing itself that American plumbing,
> . . . farm implements and a thousand other
> things have become notable in the world. Yet
> we are timid in believing that in the arts
> discovery and invention will take the same
> course.

Poe's views are sufficiently similar to support the notion that "Mr.
Griswold and the Poets" may have served as the inspiration for at least
a part of "Yours, O Youth."

> The idiosyncrasy of our political posi-
> tion has stimulated into early action what-
> ever practical talent we possessed. . . .
> But the arena of exertion, and of consequent
> distinction, into which our first and most
> obvious wants impelled us, has been regarded
> as the field of our deliberate choice. Our
> necessities have been taken for our propen-
> sities. . . . Because we are not all Homers
> in the beginning, it has been somewhat rash-
> ly taken for granted that we shall be all
> Jeremy Benthams in the end.

What Poe did as a writer, in Williams' opinion, was to carry over
"the truest instinct in America," namely "to HAVE the world or leave it,"
into his work as an artist. In short, Poe translated--and was the first
to do so in Williams' mind--American drives for excellence and exactitude
into words. He was the kind of original craftsman that built America's
material greatness, using his craft to produce instead a spiritual expression of himself and his surroundings. "Lowell, Bryant, etc., concerned poetry with literature," writes Williams, "Poe concerned it with
the soul; hence their differing conceptions of the use of language." As
in Williams' own best writing, Poe's "words [are] not hung by usage with
associations, the pleasing wraiths of former masteries. . . ."

The parallels between Poe and Williams--and Lowell, Bryant and Long-

fellow and many of Williams' most famous contemporaries--while they do
not intrude directly into the chapter, nonetheless provide it with some
formidable resonances. And many of the qualities and methods in Poe's
writing that Williams singles out in this essay give us insights into his
own aims and intentions at this point in his career. Both men certainly
exhibit, as Williams writes of Poe, "an anger to sweep out the unorigi-
nal .... to annihilate the copied, the slavish, the FALSE literature"
that surrounds them. Both men felt that, as Williams quotes Poe, a writer
who wishes to communicate his ideas intelligibly "'should employ those
forms of speech which are best adapted to further his object. He should
speak to the people in that people's ordinary tongue.'" This is certainly the essence of Williams' best writing as a poet; and in the prose, as
we have seen, he frequently shows the same simplicity, coupled with what
he refers to later as Poe's "primitive awkwardness of diction, lack of
polish, colloquialism."

    In Poe's hands, as in Williams' when he is at his best, "the particles
of language" are "as clear as sand." Moreover the language used by both
men represents "a remarkable HISTORY of the locality" inhabited by each.
Williams' admiration for Poe's ability to let his method show through his
writing, to convey a sense of power and magnetism by sheer technique--the
attractiveness of the mind at work--is related to his own achievements in
Kora in Hell. As we have a keen sense of Williams' real and fantasied
life in rural New Jersey in the second decade of the century from the improvisations of Kora so, as he writes, "the whole period, America 1840,
could be rebuilt, psychologically (phrenologically) from Poe's 'method'."
In Williams' attachment to the local conditions of northern New Jersey

we sense that, like Poe, he "conceived the possibility, the sullen, vol-
canic inevitability of the place." And as he used mythic and non-local
material--for the first time in Kora, but elsewhere throughout his work,
most notably in Paterson--to give a new dimension to his locale, so he
saw Poe as "using every tool France, England, Greece could give him,--
but [using] them to original purpose."

The major difference between the two is perhaps in their choice of
materials for their art. For Poe this material was, as Williams correctly points out, "abstract," as Williams seldom is. Moreover, and this despite Williams' extensive and complicated disclaimer, Poe's attention was
as much devoted to the supernatural for its own sake as it was because
the supernatural served to clip away "the 'scenery' near at hand in order
to let the real business of composition show." The fact remains, however,
that in Poe, Williams finds as close a thing to a spiritual and artistic
ancestor as he does anywhere in In the American Grain.

He had intended the Poe chapter to be the last of the book--presum-
ably something of a cap-stone. His editor, however, insisted that he include a piece on Lincoln, and Williams complied. The essay is chiefly memorable because in Williams' hands Lincoln becomes the embodiment of the
maternal rather than the impossibly masculine "Great Railsplitter." He
compares Lincoln to the Dutch conductor Mengelberg, "a great broad hipped
one," who leads an orchestra as if he were "a woman drawing to herself
with insatiable passion the myriad points of sound, conferring upon each
the dignity of a successful approach, relieving each of his swelling burden (but particularly, by himself), in the overtowering symphony. . . ."
This is an awkward and infelicitous comparison, to say the least, but

somehow Williams almost makes it work, conjuring up the image of Lincoln as "a woman in an old shawl--with a great bearded face and a towering black hat above it, to give unearthly reality." The treatment is finally somewhat ludicrous, and this is sad because In the American Grain thus ends on a faltering note with a chapter that is a notable anti-climax after the splendid one on Poe.

For Williams, radically willing, as Horace Gregory later wrote, "to accept the limitations of normal growth,"[29] In the American Grain was an extremely important moment in his development. It exhibits a richer sense of identity, and a greater control of tone and style than any of the earlier prose work of the Contact years; and taken together with the improvisations of Kora in Hell, it is perhaps the clearest prose indication from these years of Williams' stature as a writer. But the improvisations are something of a laboratory and In the American Grain is not. It retains the familiar impressionism and presents us often with the vision of method working out through material. But it is the product of mature and careful consideration for the most part, as well as a great deal of study. It is in no way a really erudite book, but it is full of the sense of what it was to be an intelligent and curious man living in America at the time of its writing, and it is also full of Williams' own unique characteristics as a man and as an artist.

The writing of In the American Grain marked the end of the "early" period of Williams' prose. In the book he consolidated most of the ideas about the American experience and the role of the American artist that had occurred to him during the first fifteen years of his creative life. In dealing with figures he considered representative of the major features of

American life, he found points of focus for his own experience and thought that were to serve as the basis for his best work--both prose and poetry-- until the end of his life. Kora in Hell and The Great American Novel had served as an exploration of the way the artist's mind works, and the Contact essays and Spring and All as a presentation of a coherent critical stance; In the American Grain pulled together the totality of the man's present and past experience in an attempt to identify what was unique in being an American of special talent and how such a man might relate to his fellow Americans.

Over the ensuing years Williams was to experiment with prose continuously. But the direction of his mind was already established and his course set by 1925. He had explored various prose styles and aims and chosen those he wished to make his own. If his critical writing became more erudite and less angry as time went on, that was a product of increasing maturity on his part and a gradual lessening of the pressures of neglect and indifference under which he felt he and his friends had to work. He had already discovered the importance of his environment--of "the local" --and he was to rely on this throughout the rest of his career.

Williams' task as a writer was to be, as James Guimond has put it, "a discovery and possession of America."[30] He never deviated from this purpose, though he varied his exploratory techniques somewhat over his lifetime. The other side of that task was, of course, the discovery and possession of William Carlos Williams, American. In A Voyage to Pagany (1928), this identity is examined in the context of Williams' European journey of 1924, through the persona of Dev Evans. In the stories of A Knife of the Times (1932) and in those that followed, Williams sought repeatedly to define what it was that was unique about the American locality and experience and, equally important, what was unique about the way in which he himself saw and expressed these realities. The crowning achievement of his career as a poet and prose writer is <u>Paterson</u>, in which the prose is used chiefly to provide the "facts," the background against which the poetry becomes a moving and operable communication of the state of a man's mind within his immediate environment. It is with the internal and external "facts" of his existence that Williams was concerned as a writer of prose from the beginning. He defined his intentions and his directions between 1917 and 1925.

Footnotes

Introduction

1. Books on Williams have begun to appear on the market in increasing numbers. Linda W. Wagner's The Prose of Williams Carlos Williams (Middletown, Conn.: Wesleyan University Press, 1970) and James E. Breslin's William Carlos Williams: An American Artist (New York: Oxford University Press, 1970) have come out too recently to be treated in my dissertation. Williams' own work has also been coming back into print after years of neglect. Spring and All (West Newbury, Mass.: Frontier Press, 1970) and Imaginations, ed. Webster Schott (New York: New Directions, 1970) have made available to the general reader all of Williams' early and important prose work.

Chapter One

1. In a letter from Crane to Williams quoted in John Unterecker, Voyager: A Life of Hart Crane (New York: Farrar, Straus and Giroux, 1969), p. 559.

2. William Rose Benét, Fifty Poets: An American Auto-Anthology (New York: Duffield and Green, 1933), p. 60.

3. "A Selection from The Tempers. By William Carlos Williams. With Introductory Note by Ezra Pound." The Poetry Review, London, I, No. 10 (Oct. 1912), 481-84. The Tempers was printed in London in 1913 by Elkin Mathews, thanks also to Pound's intervention.

4. In his Autobiography (New York: Random House, 1951), pp. 158-59, Williams writes that he paid "something in the neighborhood of two hundred and fifty dollars" for each of the three books printed by The Four Seas Company (Al Que Quiere, Kora in Hell and Sour Grapes). But he says in I Wanted to Write a Poem, Reported and Edited by Edith Heal (Boston: Beacon Press, 1958), p. 18, that Al Que Quiere "took $50 out of my pocket. . . . No, it was more than $50, but some of the money could be considered toward my fourth book, Sour Grapes, which the Four Seas Company published with no further donation from me."

5. "The Great Opportunity--New York Letter," The Egoist, III, No. 9 (Sept. 1916), 137. The letter also appears in Selected Letters, ed. John C. Thirlwall (New York: McDowell, Obolensky, 1957) pp. 30-33, incorrectly dated 1915.

6. "The Great Sex Spiral, A Criticism of Miss Marsden's 'Lingual Psychology,'" The Egoist, IV, No. 3 (April 1917), 46, and IV, No. 7 (Aug. 1917), 110-11.

7. One is reminded here that Williams was himself not a drinker, as he says several times in the Autobiography. The drunkenness he talks of here is related rather to the spirit of such a poem as "Danse Russe" in which the intoxication experienced by the dancer is that of a man alone with himself and his creativity. See "Danse Russe," Collected Earlier Poems of William Carlos Williams (New York: New Directions, 1966), p. 148. Words were Williams' alcohol.

8. "The Delicacies," The Egoist, IV, No. 9 (Oct. 1917), 137.

9. See The Build-up (New York: New Directions, 1968), Chapter 18.

10. "America, Whitman, and the Art of Poetry," The Poetry Journal, VII, No. 1 (Nov. 1917), 27-36.

11. This statement was made by Williams in the year that T. S. Eliot's The Love Song of J. Alfred Prufrock appeared. It is only one indication of the gulf between Williams and Eliot which existed from the very beginning of their careers.

12. Williams' spelling is often, frankly, atrocious. Rather than burden the reader with a parade of "sics," I will hereafter correct the most obvious errors. One reason for Williams' mistakes is perhaps his familiarity with several languages and a resultant confusion among them from time to time. Another is simple carelessness.

13. Pound took Williams to see the National Gallery when Williams visited him in London in 1910, so Williams' knowledge of Turner was presumably, in part at least, first hand.

14. "Prose About Love," The Little Review, VI [V], No. 2 (June 1918), 5-10.

15. "The Ideal Quarrel," The Little Review, V, No. 8 (Dec. 1918), 39-40; "The Man Who Resembled a Horse," ibid., 42-53.

16. "The Professional Studies," The Little Review, V, Nos. 10-11 (Feb.-March 1919), 36-44.

17. Williams' views on Joyce changed significantly over the next several years, as we shall see.

18. This subdued and serious personality is quite different, for example, from the privately intoxicated one revealed in "Danse Russe," or, for that matter, in several of the improvisations of Kora in Hell, to be discussed later.

19. "The Comic Life of Elia Brobitza," Others, V, No. 5 (April-May 1919), 1-16.

20. In some ways this play is a direct ancestor of Williams' later "A Dream of Love," first produced in 1949 and available in Many Loves and Other Plays (New York: New Directions, 1961), pp. 105-223. Both plays revolve around the ghostly reappearance of male lovers to women whose lives are going to pieces. But the earlier work draws some of its inspiration, I would suggest, from the figure of Williams' grandmother, Emily Dickinson, whose maiden name is not unlike that of the central character; while the later play is unflinchingly autobiographical for the most part and deals with Williams' own marriage and his imagined death.

21. Six letters from Williams to Miss Lowell are reprinted in Selected Letters. Her letters to him are in the Houghton Library, Harvard University.

22. There is a dating problem involved here. Williams' letter of congratulation on "Appuldurcombe Park" is dated August 7, 1918 in Selected Letters. But her letter in response is also dated August 7 (n. d.). Possibly Miss Lowell was in error, but that is unlike her.

23. Others, V, No. 6 (July 1919). Williams was fond of Carnevali and took him under his wing. For a fuller account of their relationship see the Autobiography, pp. 266-69. Those interested in Carnevali's fortunes after he returned to Europe will find an intimate portrait in Robert McAlmon and Kay Boyle, Being Geniuses Together 1920-1930 (New York: Doubleday and Co., 1968).

24. Williams had already made use of that "curt answer" in another context in the first part of the Prologue to Kora in Hell, published in April as "Prologue: the Return of the Sun," in The Little Review, V, No. 12, 1-16.

25. Williams must have started work on "The Discovery of the Indies"--the Columbus chapter of In the American Grain in late 1922. It first appeared in Broom, Berlin, IV, No. 4 (March 1923), 252-60. But it is clear that he was thinking seriously about major figures in the American tradition at least as early as his essay on Whitman, discussed earlier.

26. "A Maker," The Little Review, VI, No. 4 (Aug. 1919), 37-39.

27. By 1929, Williams was no longer as enthusiastic about Gould's work. "From Queens to Cats," in The Dial, LXXXVI, No. 1 (Jan. 1929), 66-67, a review of Gould's Aphrodite and Other Poems by Williams is not at all encouraging.

28. "More Swill," The Little Review, VI, No. 6 (Oct. 1919), 29-30.

Chapter Two

1. <u>The Little Review</u>, Chicago, IV, No. 6 (Oct. 1917), 19.

2. <u>Kora in Hell</u> (Boston: The Four Seas Co., 1920), p. 29. All subsequent quotations from <u>Kora in Hell</u> refer to this text unless otherwise noted.

3. Maxwell Bodenheim, "Style and American Literature," <u>The Little Review</u>, IV, No. 6 (Oct. 1917), 24.

4. <u>Autobiography</u>, p. 158. Williams said later that "The book was composed backward. The Improvisations which I have told you about came first; then the Interpretations which appear below the dividing line." <u>I Wanted to Write a Poem</u>, p. 29.

5. <u>The Little Review</u>, VI, No. 2 (June 1919), 52-59.

6. <u>I Wanted to Write a Poem</u>, p. 27.

7. Ibid., p. 26.

8. <u>Kora in Hell</u> (San Francisco: City Lights Books, 1957), p. 6.

9. "Kora in Hell by William Carlos Williams," <u>Contact</u>, New York, 4 (Summer,1921), 5-8. Reprinted in <u>William Carlos Williams</u>, ed. J. Hillis Miller (Englewood Cliffs, N. J.: Prentice-Hall, 1966), pp. 37-41.

10. Quoted in John Unterecker, <u>Voyager</u>, p. 190.

11. Williams' translation of the Spanish, as he says in <u>I Wanted to Write a Poem</u>, p. 19, was "To Him Who Wants It."

12. <u>I Wanted to Write a Poem</u>, p. 30.

13. Although "The Shadow" was not printed in a collection until 1938 in <u>The Complete Collected Poems</u> (Norfolk: New Directions), it first appeared in print in <u>Poetry</u>, VI, No. 2 (May 1915), 62.

14. Kora, or Kore, was Persephone's cult name as she figured in the Eleusinian mysteries.

15. <u>I Wanted to Write a Poem</u>, p. 29.

16. <u>Kora in Hell</u> (San Francisco: City Lights Books, 1957), p. 5.

17. <u>I Wanted to Write a Poem</u>, p. 30.

18. Ibid., p. 16.

19. Williams' mother had been an art student as a young woman, and as he notes in the Autobiography, p. 15, she also had "among her intimates" the reputation of being a "medium." She actually experienced spiritual trances or "visitations" during Williams' youth.

20. "Kora in Hell by William Carlos Williams," p. 7.

21. The passage quoted by Miss Moore is from the interpretation or explanation to Improvisation XIX. 3.

22. The Armory Show in New York in 1913 had a stimulating effect on American art, as is well known. Williams remembered in the Autobiography, in the chapter "Painters and Parties" (pp. 134-142), especially the impact of Duchamps and his own reading of "Overture to a Dance of Locomotives" and "Portrait of a Woman in Bed," which at least one member of the audience walked out on.

23. I Wanted to Write a Poem, p. 31.

24. Ibid. The notion of linking himself with great writers of the past goes back in Williams at least as far as the epigraphs to his Poems (Rutherford: privately printed, 1909), which were from Keats and Shakespeare. But one has the feeling that in Kora, it was at least partly in imitation of the very writers--Pound and Eliot--at whom he directs his most blistering attacks in the Prologue.

25. The attacks roused Pound and elicited from him a somewhat backhanded defense of Jepson. He wrote to Williams, "That Jep. is not a fountain of wisdom I admit, but he was a good bolus (or a bad bolus). But at any rate there was no one else whose time wasn't too valuable to waste on trying to penetrate Harriet's [Harriet Monroe] crest." The Letters of Ezra Pound, ed. D. D. Paige (New York: Harcourt, Brace and World, 1950), p. 157. Jepson had written an attack on Poetry's 1916 prizes and Williams' Prologue is in part, as Paige points out, a direct response to that attack.

26. I Wanted to Write a Poem, p. 30.

27. Autobiography, p. 174.

28. Williams' personal dislike as distinct from his artistic dislike of Eliot probably erupted finally in 1924 when Eliot politely refused to print Williams' article on Marianne Moore in Criterion.

29. I Wanted to Write a Poem, p. 31.

30. "Demuth" is, of course, Williams' old and close friend, the American Precisionist painter Charles Demuth.

31. Williams writes in the Prologue that "when Margaret Anderson published my first improvisations Ezra Pound wrote me one of his hurried letters in which he urged me to give some hint by which the reader of good will might come at my intention" (Kora, p. 13).

32. _Autobiography_, p. 158.

33. _I Wanted to Write a Poem_, p. 30.

34. I do not mean to suggest that absolutely hard and fast distinctions among these types of improvisations can be drawn. More often than not an improvisation will contain elements of all of these, though one seems generally to predominate over the others as the author's chief momentary intention. In my discussion I shall try to focus on examples of those types of work which will best serve to illustrate the nature of the book as a whole and the associational mode of progressing employed by Williams as he improvises. My desire is not to canvass the book but to convey a sense of the writer's mind at work in his first major attempt at experimental prose and to flesh out the text with appropriate biographical data or reference to other improvisations or works where possible or relevant. I shall refer to each piece by its roman and arabic numbering in the original text.

35. _Autobiography_, p. 112.

36. The improvisation has richer resonances if one considers the "late loiterer" to be related to Pluto, another late loiterer of summer, and the old woman and the girl to be similarly related to Demeter and Persephone.

37. _The Inferno_, Canto XXXIV, 136-39.

38. _I Wanted to Write a Poem_, pp. 27-28.

39. One recalls here Dryden's peculiarly infelicitous description of Lord Hastings, ravaged by smallpox, "whose corpse might seem a _constellation_." ("Upon the Death of Lord Hastings," 1. 66)

40. The improvisation was published almost a year before his father's death, in _The Little Review_, V, No. 9 [should be IV.9] (Jan. 1918), without any interpretive section.

41. _Autobiography_, p. 166.

42. The mention of October brings to mind "the autumn weather" of Wallace Stevens' poem "Le Monocle de Mon Oncle," first published in December, 1918.

Chapter Three

1. Unsigned editorial, _Contact_, New York, [No. 1] (Dec. 1920), 1.

2. "Further Announcement," ibid., 10. This may have been written by McAlmon, though it sounds very much like Williams. It is not listed in Emily Mitchell Wallace, _A Bibliography of William Carlos Williams_ (Middletown: Wesleyan Univ. Press, 1968).

3. _Autobiography_, p. 391.

4. Marsden Hartley, "The Red Man," _Adventures in the Arts_ (New York: Boni and Liveright, 1921), pp. 13-29.

5. "A Matisse," _Contact_, [No. 2] (Jan. 1921), [1]. This essay has been reprinted in _Selected Essays of William Carlos Williams_ (New York: Random House, 1954) and _The William Carlos Williams Reader_, ed. M. L. Rosenthal (New York: New Directions, 1966).

6. "Comment," _Contact_, [No. 2] (Jan. 1921), [11-12]. The essay has been reprinted in _Selected Essays_.

7. This evaluation of Joyce is in marked contrast to Williams' earlier dismissal of his technique as "childish--Victrola," in "Three Professional Studies," discussed in my first chapter.

8. "Yours, O Youth," _Contact_, [No. 3], [Spring 1921], 14-16. The essay has been reprinted in _Selected Essays_. The charges were made by Thomas Jewell Craven, but my research has failed to ascertain when or where he advanced them.

9. _Autobiography_, p. 15.

10. _Selected Letters_, pp. 50-51.

11. William Carlos Williams, _A Voyage to Pagany_ (New York: The Macaulay Co., 1928).

12. Ibid., pp. 32-34.

13. During 1922, Williams published twelve poems in various magazines and an essay in _The Little Review_, IX, 3 [should be IX, 1] (Autumn 1922), 59-60, entitled "Reader Critic," praising the magazine.

14. "Glorious Weather," _Contact_, No. 5 (June 1923), [1-5].

15. _Autobiography_, p. 174.

16. Ibid.

Chapter Four

1. William Carlos Williams, _The Great American Novel_ (Paris: Three Mountains Press, 1923). Reprinted in _American Short Novels_, ed. R. P. Blackmur (New York: Thomas Y. Crowell Co., 1960), pp. 307-43. I have used the latter text.

2. _Autobiography_, p. 237.

3. _I Wanted to Write a Poem_, p. 38.

4. Hugh Kenner, "A Note on The Great American Novel," William Carlos Williams, ed. J. Hillis Miller (Englewood Cliffs, N. J.: Prentice-Hall, Inc., 1966), pp. 88-92. But it should be pointed out that the editor and printer of the Contact series may have had something to do with this typographical sight-gag.

5. Leslie Fiedler, Love and Death in the American Novel, rev. ed. (New York: Stein & Day, 1966), p. 24.

6. In a letter to Kenneth Burke written on March 26, 1924 from Rome (Selected Letters, pp. 60-62), Williams deals with the opening of The Great American Novel. "Yes, my Great American Novel never found a beginning. It was that I must have wanted to say. . . . It's got to be said to be read. I am trying to speak, to tell it in the only way possible--but I do want to say what there is. It is not for me merely to arrange things prettily."

7. Autobiography, pp. 267-68.

8. "Danse Pseudomacabre," The Little Review, VII, No. 1 (May-June 1920), 46-49. Reprinted in William Carlos Williams, The Farmers' Daughters (New York: New Directions, 1961), pp. 208-11.

9. In his chapter "Edgar Allan Poe" in In the American Grain (New Directions, 1956), pp. 216-33, Williams deals with a writer whose work appeared "new to the French." They found Poe's work, in Williams' words, "a new point from which to readjust the trigonometric measurements of literary form" (p. 216).

10. Both Williams and Masters were included, however, in Ezra Pound's Catholic Anthology (London: Elkin Mathews, 1915) and again in Pound's Profile (Milan: John Scheiwiller, 1932).

11. In 1923 Williams was himself forty years old.

Chapter Five

1. I Wanted to Write a Poem, p. 37.

2. In the Autobiography (p. 52), Williams writes, "I met Charles Demuth over a dish of prunes at Mrs. Chain's boarding house on Locust Street and formed a lifelong friendship on the spot with dear Charlie, now long since dead."

3. James Guimond, The Art of William Carlos Williams (Urbana: Univ. of Illinois Press, 1968), esp. pp. 41-64.

4. Ibid., p. 43.

5. William Carlos Williams, <u>Spring</u> <u>and</u> <u>All</u> (Dijon: Contact Publishing Co., 1923). Reprinted complete recently by The Frontier Press, Newbury, Mass., 1970 and in <u>Imaginations</u> ed. Webster Schott (New York: New Directions, 1970). My text is that of the original edition.

6. William Carlos Williams, <u>Collected</u> <u>Poems</u> <u>1921</u>-<u>1931</u> (New York: The Objectivist Press, 1934).

7. Williams makes these remarks in <u>I</u> <u>Wanted</u> <u>to</u> <u>Write</u> <u>a</u> <u>Poem</u>, p. 52.

8. Ibid., p. 36.

9. Loc. cit.

10. W. B. Yeats, "The Fisherman," <u>The</u> <u>Collected</u> <u>Poems</u> (New York: Macmillan, 1960), p. 145.

11. I am following here a suggestion made by Hillis Miller in the chapter "Prose from Spring and All," in <u>William</u> <u>Carlos</u> <u>Williams</u> (p. 17n). The original text reads "The inevitable flux of the seeing eye toward measuring itself by the world it inhabits can only result in himself crushing humiliation unless the individual raise to some approximate co-extension with the universe. . . ."

12. The notion advanced here by Williams is related to the "snapper" technique employed in <u>Kora</u>: the detaching of simple things, events, people from ordinary experience by means of a sudden imaginative leap.

13. <u>Autobiography</u>, p. 240.

14. Loc. cit.

15. Ibid., p. 241.

16. James Joyce, "Aesthetics, The Paris Notebook," <u>The</u> <u>Critical</u> <u>Writings</u> <u>of</u> <u>James</u> <u>Joyce</u>, ed. Ellsworth Mason and Richard Ellmann (New York: Viking, 1959), p. 145.

17. Not only is it not Shakespeare, it is Hamlet (<u>Hamlet</u>, III. ii. 1-15) who gives us the advice, and the sense of the speech is that <u>theatre</u> ("playing") holds up the mirror, not art generally.

18. Williams certainly had something of a reputation as a man about town, if we are to trust the <u>Dial</u>. "Comment," <u>Dial</u>, 71, No. 1 (July 1921), 123-26, sarcastically attacks the Ellerman-McAlmon marriage. In the course of things Williams himself ("the bouncing apple of how many satined boudoirs?") comes under the knife.

19. Marsden Hartley, "The Importance of Being 'Dada'," <u>Adventures</u> <u>in</u> <u>the</u> <u>Arts</u> (New York: Boni and Liveright, 1921), pp. 249, 254.

Chapter Six

1. Pound had urged such a trip when he was trying to get Williams to contribute to the "Bel Esprit" effort to subsidize Eliot in 1922. He offered to back Williams as the second recipient of the "grant" and went on to say, "I think you ought to have a year off or a six months' vacation in Europe. I think you are afraid to take it, for fear of destroying some illusions which you think necessary to your illusions. I don't think you ought to leave permanently, your job gives you too real a contact, too valuable to give up. BUT you ought to see a human being now and again" (The Letters of Ezra Pound, p. 173).

2. "The Destruction of Tenochtitlan," Broom, Berlin, IV, 2 (Jan. 1922 [should be 1923]), 112-20. "The Discoverers: I. Red Eric," Broom, Berlin, IV, 3 (Feb. 1923), 182-86. "The Discovery of the Indies," Broom, Berlin, IV, 4 (March 1923), 252-60. Reprinted, with changes in In the American Grain (New York: New Directions, 1964), which is the text I have used in my discussion.

3. Autobiography, p. 178.

4. I Wanted to Write a Poem, p. 43.

5. Selected Letters, p. 69.

6. Autobiography, p. 178.

7. James Guimond, The Art of William Carlos Williams, p. 92.

8. Frederick J. Hoffman, The Twenties (New York: The Free Press, 1965), p. 162.

9. Guimond, p. 83.

10. In I Wanted to Write a Poem, Williams says, "Obviously I couldn't imitate the Norse but I chose a style that was barbaric and primitive, as I knew Eric the Red to be" (p. 42).

11. Williams had apparently started White Mule, the first novel in the trilogy, based on what he knew of his wife's infancy and childhood, as early as 1923. In A Return to Pagany, ed. Stephen Halpert with Richard Johns (Boston: Beacon Press, 1969), p. 127, a letter from Williams to Johns, unpublished elsewhere, dated June 5, 1930, says, "You have greatly encouraged me to go on with the thing [White Mule]--after a seven years' interval."

12. The theme of turning inland toward fresh discoveries runs throughout Paterson. See especially the end of Book IV in which the man (Paterson himself) who had been swimming "picked/some beach plums from a low bush and/ sampled one of them, spitting the seed out,/then headed inland, followed

by the dog." William Carlos Williams, Paterson (New York: New Directions, 1963), pp. 237-38. The turn inland is one made in another sense by Poe in In the American Grain, and typified by Daniel Boone's conquest of Kentucky.

13. I Wanted to Write a Poem, p. 42.

14. See Charles Olson, "The Kingfishers," The Distances (New York: Grove Press, 1960), pp. 5-11, and also The Mayan Letters (London: Jonathan Cape Ltd., 1968).

15. One reason for Montezuma's passivity was that he and his people believed Cortez and the Spaniards to be gods led by the great emperor god Quetzalcoatl, returning to their people. By extraordinary chance Cortez' invasion came at precisely the time that this return had been predicted. Apparently Montezuma clung to this interpretation even after the greed of the Spaniards had exposed them as all too human. For a full discussion of the Quetzalcoatl myth and the conquest of the Aztecs see George C. Vaillant, The Aztecs of Mexico rev. ed. (Garden City, N. Y.: Doubleday, 1962).

16. I Wanted to Write a Poem, p. 43.

17. D. H. Lawrence, Studies in Classic American Literature (New York: Viking, 1961), p. 57.

18. Selden Rodman, One Hundred Modern Poems (New York: Pellegrini and Cudahy, 1949), pp. 94-98. Williams' letter to Rodman about the piece, dated Nov. 14, 1949, is in Selected Letters, pp. 275-76.

19. For a full discussion of attitudes toward the Puritans in the 1920's, see Hoffman, The Twenties, pp. 355-69.

20. Quoted in Hoffman, pp. 355-56.

21. Robert Lowell retells the tale in "Endecott and the Red Cross," The Old Glory (New York: Farrar, Straus and Giroux, 1965), pp. 1-59.

22. Williams mentions only his first "six weeks in Paris" at the beginning of the chapter (In the American Grain, p. 105). He was evidently much moved by the conversation with Larbaud as two letters to Marianne Moore make clear (Selected Letters, pp. 59-60 and 62-63).

23. Selected Letters, p. 60.

24. Ibid., p. 63.

25. Williams was still intrigued with Boone after the completion of In the American Grain. In a prose-poem "Insanity or Genius," printed in The Little Review, New York, XII, No. 1 (Spring-Summer 1926), 10, "Daniel Boone, the father of Kentucky" heads a long list of "interests of 1926."

The poem was subsequently retitled "Interests of 1926" in Collected Earlier Poems.

26. Autobiography, p. 183 and I Wanted to Write a Poem, p. 43.

27. He does so in the "Beautiful Thing" sections of Paterson. In other stories, like "The Colored Girls of Passenack--Old and New" in The Farmers' Daughters, Williams is very much the prisoner of his ambivalence and prejudice. In the Autobiography (p. 12) he tells us that his family's black maid, Georgie, was one of the first women he saw without clothes. He and other children "took turns peeking through a hole in the wall of her attic bedroom."

28. Guimond, p. 88.

29. Horace Gregory, "Introduction," In the American Grain, [p. vii].

30. The sub-title of Guimond's book is A Discovery and Possession of America.

174

A Selected Bibliography

Works by William Carlos Williams

Williams, William Carlos. Al Que Quiere! Boston: The Four Seas Co., 1917.

--------. "America, Whitman, and the Art of Poetry." The Poetry Journal, VII (Nov. 1917), 27-36.

--------. The Autobiography. New York: Random House, 1951.

--------. A Beginning on the Short Story. Yonkers: The Alicat Bookshop Press, 1950.

--------. "Belly Music." Others, V (July 1919), 25-32.

--------. The Collected Earlier Poems. New York: New Directions, 1966.

--------. The Collected Later Poems. Norfolk, Conn.: New Directions, 1963.

--------. Collected Poems 1921-1931. Preface by Wallace Stevens. New York: The Objectivist Press, 1934.

--------. "The Comic Life of Elia Brobitza." Others, V (April-May 1919), 1-16.

--------. "Comment." Contact, [No. 2] (Jan. 1921), [11-12].

--------. "Danse Pseudomacabre." The Little Review, VII (May-June 1920), 46-49.

--------. "The Delicacies." The Egoist, IV (Oct. 1917), 137.

--------. "The Discovery of the Indies." Broom, Berlin, IV (March 1923), 252-60.

--------. The Farmers' Daughters. Norfolk, Conn.: New Directions, 1961.

--------. "From Queens to Cats." The Dial, LXXXVI (Jan. 1929), 66-67.

--------. "Further Announcement." Contact, [No. 1] (Dec. 1920), 10.

--------. "Gloria!" Others, V (July 1919), 3-4.

--------. "Glorious Weather." Contact, No. 5 (June 1923), [1-5].

--------. The Great American Novel. Paris: Three Mountains Press, 1923.

--------. "The Great Opportunity--New York Letter." The Egoist, III (Sept. 1916), 137.

-------. "The Great Sex Spiral, A Criticism of Miss Marsden's 'Lingual Psychology.'" The Egoist, IV (April 1917), 46 and IV (Aug 1917), 110-11.

-------. I Wanted to Write a Poem. Ed. Edith Heal, Boston: Beacon Press, 1967.

-------. "The Ideal Quarrel." The Little Review, V (Dec. 1918), 39-40.

-------. "Improvisations." The Little Review, IV (Oct. 1917), 19 also V [IV] (Jan. 1918), 3-9 and VI (June 1919), 52-59.

-------. In the American Grain. New York: New Directions, 1964.

-------. In the Money. New York: New Directions, 1967.

-------. Kora in Hell: Improvisations. Boston: The Four Seas Co., 1920 also published by City Lights Books, San Francisco, 1957.

-------. "A Maker." The Little Review, VI (Aug. 1919), 37-39.

-------. "A Man Versus the Law." The Freeman, I (June 23, 1920), 348-49.

-------. "The Man Who Resembled a Horse." The Little Review, V (Dec. 1918), 42-53.

-------. Many Loves and Other Plays. Norfolk, Conn.: New Directions, 1961.

-------. "A Matisse." Contact, [No. 2] (Jan. 1921), [1].

-------. "More Swill." The Little Review, VI (Oct. 1919), 29-30.

-------. A Novelette and Other Prose (1921-1931). Toulon: To Publishers, 1932.

-------. Paterson. New York: New Directions, 1963.

-------. "Prologue: the Return of the Sun." The Little Review, V (April 1919), 1-16.

-------. "Prologue to a Book of Improvisations, Kora in Hell, Now Being Published by the Four Seas Company." The Little Review, VI (May 1919), 74-80.

-------. "Prose About Love." The Little Review, IV [V] (June 1918), 5-10.

-------. "Reader Critic." The Little Review, IX (Autumn 1922), 59-60.

-------. Selected Essays. New York: Random House, 1954.

--------. The Selected Letters. Ed. John C. Thirlwall. New York: Mc-
Dowell, Obolensky, 1957.

--------. Selected Poems. New York: New Directions, 1963.

--------. "A Selection from the Tempers." With Introductory Note by Ezra
Pound. The Poetry Review, London, I (Oct. 1912), 481-84.

--------. Sour Grapes. Boston: The Four Seas Co., 1921.

--------. Spring and All. Paris: Contact Publishing Co., 1923.

--------. The Tempers. London: Elkin Mathews, 1913.

--------. "Three Professional Studies." The Little Review, V (Feb.-March
1919), 36-44.

--------. Unsigned editorial. Contact, [No. 1] (Dec. 1920), 1.

--------. A Voyage to Pagany. New York: The Macaulay Co., 1928.

--------. White Mule. New York: New Directions, 1967.

--------. The William Carlos Williams Reader. Ed. M. L. Rosenthal. New
York: New Directions, 1966.

--------. Yes, Mrs. Williams. New York: McDowell, Obolensky, 1959.

--------. "Yours, O Youth." Contact, [No. 3] [Spring 1921], 14-16.

Other Works Consulted

American Short Novels. Ed. R. P. Blackmur. New York: Thomas Y. Crowell
Co., 1960.

Anon. "Comment." The Dial, LXXI (July 1921), 23-26.

Benét, William Rose. Fifty Poets: An American Auto-Anthology. New York:
Duffield and Green, 1933.

Bodenheim, Maxwell. "Style and American Literature." The Little Review,
IV (Oct. 1917), 22-24.

Briarcliff Quarterly, III (Oct. 1946), "William Carlos Williams Number."

Brinnin, John Malcolm. William Carlos Williams. Minneapolis: University
of Minnesota Press, 1963.

Catholic Anthology. Ed. Ezra Pound. London: Elkin Mathews, 1915.

The Critical Writings of James Joyce. Ed. Ellsworth Mason and Richard Ellmann. New York: Viking, 1959.

Eliot, T. S. Collected Poems, 1909-1962. New York: Harcourt, Brace and World, 1963.

Fiedler, Leslie. Love and Death in the American Novel. rev. ed. New York: Stein and Day, 1966.

"A Gathering for William Carlos Williams." The Massachusetts Review, III (Winter 1962), 277-344.

Guimond, James. The Art of William Carlos Williams: A Discovery and Possession of America. Urbana: University of Illinois Press, 1968.

Hartley, Marsden. Adventures in the Arts. New York: Boni and Liveright, 1921.

Hoffman Frederick J. The Twenties: American Writing in the Postwar Decade. New York: The Free Press, 1965.

Koch, Vivienne. William Carlos Williams. Norfolk, Conn.: New Directions, 1950.

Lawrence, D. H. Studies in Classic American Literature. New York: Viking, 1961.

The Letters of Ezra Pound. Ed. D. D. Paige. New York: Harcourt, Brace and World, 1950.

Lowell, Robert. The Old Glory. New York: Farrar, Straus and Giroux, 1965.

Mazzaro, Jerome. "Of Love, Abiding Love." Intrepid, Buffalo, 17 (1970).

McAlmon, Robert and Kay Boyle. Being Geniuses Together 1920-1930. New York: Doubleday and Co., 1968.

Miller, J. Hillis. Poets of Reality. Cambridge, Mass.: Harvard University Press, 1965.

Moore, Marianne. "Kora in Hell by William Carlos Williams." Contact, No. 4 (Summer 1921), 5-8.

Olson, Charles. The Distances. New York: Grove, 1960.

———. The Mayan Letters. London: Jonathan Cape, 1968.

Ostrum, Alan. The Poetic World of William Carlos Williams. Carbondale: Southern Illinois University Press, 1966.

<u>Profile</u>. Ed. Ezra Pound. Milan: John Scheiwiller, 1932.

<u>A Return to Pagany</u>. Ed. Stephen Halpert with Richard Johns. Boston: Beacon Press, 1969.

Rodman, Selden. <u>One Hundred Modern Poems</u>. New York: Pellegrini and Cudahy, 1949.

Slate, Joseph Evans. "William Carlos Williams, Hart Crane and 'The Virtue of History,'" <u>Texas Studies in Literature and Language</u>, VI (Winter 1965), 486-511.

Stein, Gertrude. <u>Lectures in America</u>. Boston: Beacon Press, 1957.

Stevens, Wallace. <u>Poems</u>. New York: Random House, 1959.

Stock, Noel. <u>The Life of Ezra Pound</u>. New York: Pantheon, 1970.

Unterecker, John. <u>Voyager: A Life of Hart Crane</u>. New York: Farrar, Straus and Giroux, 1969.

Wagner, Linda W. <u>The Poems of William Carlos Williams</u>. Middletown, Conn.: The Wesleyan University Press, 1964.

Wallace, Emily Mitchell. <u>A Bibliography of William Carlos Williams</u>. Middletown, Conn.: The Wesleyan University Press, 1968.

<u>William Carlos Williams: A Collection of Critical Essays</u>. Ed. J. Hillis Miller. Englewood Cliffs, N. J.: Prentice-Hall Inc., 1966.

Yeats, William Butler. <u>The Collected Poems</u>. New York: Macmillan, 1960.